El

When he is on the screen, he has this unique, almost uncanny ability to talk right into the camera so that he seems to reach out and touch people. He removes some kind of barrier. The camera is his plaything, his tool . . . his utterly relaxed attitude is indeed remarkable.

He spouts four-letter words and possible insults, but his eyes erase any misunderstandings.

He seems strangely free of fear, hate, jealousy, doubt, and suspicion . . . this is why he gets away with the outrageous things he keeps getting away with . . .

EDDIE

Eddie Murphy From A to Z

Marianne Ruuth

A STAR BOOK

published by
the Paperback Division of
W.H. Allen & Co. PLC

A Star Book
Published in 1986
by the Paperback Division of
W.H. Allen & Co. PLC
44 Hill Street, London W1X 8LB

First published in the United States of America
by Holloway House Publishing Company in 1985

Typeset in Times by Fleet Graphics, Enfield, Middlesex

Printed and bound in Great Britain by
Anchor Brendon Ltd, Tiptree, Essex

ISBN 0 352 31789 2

To Eddie Murphy's legions of fans,
among whom I am one

AWARE ALWAYS

Truth is everywhere, in everything.
—*Henry Miller*

Call it apery . . . call it mimicry, parody, echoing and re-echoing, impersonation . . . Call it a talent to really see and hear, to absorb with all senses and then reproduce with an edge, with a great helping of hilarious humour and a touch of biting satire . . .

Whatever it is, Eddie Murphy has it. Lots and lots of it.

Listen to him . . .

'I was standing outside getting ready to come in here, man, and this little old Jewish guy walked up to me and said, "Buckwheat!" And there were some brothers standing next to me and said, "What that guy call you, man? Buckwheat?" And I started thinking about it, Buckwheat and all, the Little Rascals, period . . .

'. . . I come from a predominantly black family, and I have yet to run into a relative named Buckwheat. You go to a cookout and say, "My name's Ed, what's yours?" "Oh, I'm Buckwheat, nice to meet you. Yeah, Buckwheat, that's my name. No, Buck! Buckwheat! No I ain't

7

got no last name – Buckwheat, that's it. I'm serious. I'm damn serious. You don't believe me! Ain't that right, Stymie? Here's my cousin, Stymie, over here. And I want you to meet my brother – yooo, Farina, could you come over here for a minute? Yeah, Buckwheat and Farina. Farina. Really. You know how most people are named after their father? We was named after our father's favourite breakfast. That's my little sister over there. Her name's Shredded Wheat. Then my twin brothers over there, Quisp and Quake. That's my little nephew over there – he retarded – his name is Special K. Then my big sister, she a prostitute, her name is Trix. My oldest brother, he a homosexual, his name is Lucky Charms. He over there with his friend, Fruit Loops . . . " '

Street talk, right? But highly selective street talk – as was this selection, carefully chosen for its lack of X-rated material.

He delivers up street talk that goes beyond reproduction, that is honed, challenging, sometimes provocative.

No, Eddie did not grow up in the street, but whenever he moved among people anywhere, he had a habit of really seeing and really listening.

From an early age he did what most children his age did: He watched television a lot. His family remembers the small boy in front of the set, eyes glued to the screen, intently watching. Watching? It has been said that television is passive compared to going to the movies, that you *watch* television while you *see* films.

With that definition in mind, it may be safe to say that Eddie Murphy did not 'watch' television.

'He *studied* television,' says his mother.

He looked and he listened, and he gave back as he still does. He uses a mirror, and the mirror is himself . . . face, voice, body, features, walk, sounds . . . and he shows us something that is simultaneously familiar and new, often startling, even abrasive.

8

As a little kid Eddie imitated Tom and Jerry, Laurel and Hardy, newscasters, Bugs Bunny, the Beatles, actors of every kind.

As he kept imitating, and perfecting this gift, he added a little something. One can imagine this small boy, head slightly cocked to one side, exclaiming to himself on a daily (hourly?) basis, 'Hey, man, this world is really funny! Really funny!'

What was he really like as a kid?

Not so terrific, he has said at times, claiming that in the third grade he had a potbelly, glasses with brown frames, and a bald head.

So he became the class clown ('and later the village idiot,' he says with a huge grin).

Others do not agree with this vision of little Eddie.

'He wasn't really a clown,' a schoolmate of his says. 'He was cool, though. Really cool. As if he lived inside himself . . . As if he had an inner world, different from what the rest of us knew, and as if he couldn't wait to grow up and go out and inhabit that world. Or conquer it . . . '

But he says he wasn't 'into being cool.'

He was neither a joiner nor a loner. Gangs and clubs didn't interest him. Nor did school for that matter. He looked around, and he reproduced. He was a performer, and, somehow, mysteriously, he seems to have always known this.

He began his actual performing days as an imitator. His very first stage performance took place at a youth centre when he was fifteen, and it consisted of an impersonation of soul and gospel singer Al Green.

That evening did something to him. It was as if it unified all his urges and yearnings, and made him see clearly where he was going.

He looked at the faces of the kids, his peers, in the room. He saw every face turned toward him, he read rapt attention in the eyes.

That was it!

He was caught, electrified, inspired. He knew what he was going to do with the rest of his life.

He realised who and what he was.

'I'm a performer. I'm an observer who tells what I've seen and heard . . . '

He still tends to call himself a performer rather than an actor, but what is acting?

If it is to take the essence of a fictional person, a role, a character, assimilate it, blow life into the figure and give it back to the audience with total conviction, then we have here nothing less than a consummate actor — even before he became a movie actor earning rave reviews.

Like the chameleon, he changes himself. No, he tops the chameleon. He brings to mind old Proteus from the Greek legends, the tender of the seals, the one who could change himself into any shape he pleased. Quick as lightning, he went from a proud-maned, roaring lion to a tall tree with a serpent lurking in its branches to a whiskered boar to a leopard . . . with perhaps a waterfall thrown in between.

Old Proteus would have liked Eddie Murphy.

His changes are manifold, consistent, and complete.

He has the necessary timing, precision, economy of gesture, focus, and versatility to present us with a gallery of colourful characters.

Enter Mister Robinson, the outlaw in a cardigan, a ghetto version of Public Television's benevolent Mister Rogers . . . A singsong voice with a definite bite to it . . . His Bill Cosby imitations . . . Gumby, the cartoon character from the 50's who has become a carping Catskills comic . . . The highly confused reggae star Tyrone Green, semi-illiterate and an ex-con, lionised by radical chic, as he sings 'Kill de White People' . . . The black pimp Velvet Jones who goes on television and pitches his own books with titles such as 'I Wanna Be a Ho' (and 'Ho' does not stand for a tool used in the

10

garden) . . . Little Richard Simmons, half rock 'n' roll hero, half aerobics nut, a blend of the macho and whatever is considered its opposite . . . ('Good golly, Miss Molly, you look like a *hog!*') . . . Of course, Buckwheat, one of his very earliest characters, resurrecting the pickaninny from 'Little Rascals' comedies . . . Solomon, the happy but sad bus-rider . . .

It goes on and on . . .

A late-show pitchman peddling Galactic Prophylactics and the Funeral in a Cab . . . A suburban dandy . . . An Irish priest with a brogue thicker than Irish stew . . .

Let's not forget the hairdresser Dion . . . gay as anything and willing to give his clients advice on how to handle husbands, for instance . . . Lines overheard at black movie theatres . . . The skit 'Talking Cars' (buy a car in a black area and see how it talks back at you) . . . Or the act 'Drinking Fathers' about a father who comes home dead drunk rousing kids out of beds for a rambling lecture on life . . .

He can take black stereotypes and pull them out into the light and make black audiences laugh heartily . . . He appeals to white audiences, even when he does nearly anti-white skits . . .

He can do a sketch about being hit by a car and mirror the fear by the reaction of a witness ('They yo' lips over there? I thought they was snails . . . ') . . . Or he may joke about the assassination attempts on President Reagan and the Pope and skilfully elude the hazards of tastelessness.

He offends a little, then he gives room for the releasing laughter . . . If there were anger behind these creations, it would be too much, especially for TV audiences. But in all of it, there is that impish quality. 'Hey, this is just for laughs, folks!'

He parodies Elvis Presley and Stevie Wonder and Michael Jackson with the same energy and sureness of eye and ear and muscles.

When he got a little bored on the set of the movie *Beverly Hills Cop* (movie sets are boring by definition with the built-in endless waiting between takes), Eddie Murphy amused himself by watching the director, Martin Brest, order the crew around.

He took it all in.

Then he began to imitate Brest's every gesture, every expression, every command.

'He started a succession of the most perceptive and subtle insights into me,' Brest recalls. 'What he does is give the audience an opportunity to perceive everything as perceptively as he does, and that's a thrill.'

Granted, some of his perceptions and resulting reproductions must be classified as 'rough stuff.'

Some find his sweeping irreverence quite offensive.

When he does stand-up routines, he is not cautious. It is a sort of release to him. He does whatever he wants. He plays with the audience. He brings unmentionable details into focus. There are people who like him as a movie actor but who find him a bit too vulgar on stage. But to many more, it seems, he represents a release to them, too, as he makes fun of just about everything and everybody, using a language that could make soap a hot item in many homes.

And again, there is that wide, boyish, megawatt grin and that laughter from deep inside that smooths away many a harsh edge and leaves you feeling good.

BEYOND BRILLIANCE

Here's looking at you, kid!
(Humphrey Bogart line from 'Casablanca')

Either you go crazy over him or you don't like him at all, it seems.

The majority of people love the phenomenon called Eddie Murphy.

His movies have widened and enlarged his audience.

Film critics have dug into their memory stores to come up with fresher adjectives to apply to him.

'The most popular entertainer in America today,' stated *Newsweek*.

When Eddie was twenty-one, *Newsweek* gushed: 'His talent is frightening in its amplitude.'

Its competitor *Time* had this to say recently: 'His fans – just about everyone – need no catchy titles for his movies. [From now on] just call them EDDIE V, EDDIE VI, EDDIE VII. Then watch the lines form and the smiles start to glow.'

After Eddie's first film, *48 Hrs.*, the noted (and frequently feared) film critic Pauline Kael wrote: 'At twenty-one, he has his own sleek style. Murphy doesn't imitate Pryor; he doesn't need to – he has digested him. A dapper child of the disco age, he controls the tone of his scenes with Nolte. He's in charge – or rather, his reflexes are in charge. He's as swift as a shark – a Mack-the-Knife comic – and he barely gives Nolte the time of the day. This smooth-faced kid takes over the screen . . . '

New York Magazine stated, 'Murphy is going to be a very big star.'

Critic Rex Reed (not one to mince words) raved about: ' . . . enjoying the humorous elegance with which the young comic managed to steal the whole movie in his film debut.'

Newsday commented: ' . . . Murphy establishes his credentials as a serious actor and displays the screen presence of a certifiable movie star. Murphy gives us someone to care about. He brings finesse and irony, a distinctive pleasing style, to a precision clockwork melodrama.'

In the summer of 1984, a survey was conducted on behalf of MGM/UA, Tri-Star, and Home Box Office (not including the studio that has Murphy under gilded contract, namely Paramount). Eddie Murphy was found to be the absolute top box office performer in the United States, especially so far as young audiences are concerned. It clearly indicated that, as is the case with Richard Pryor and Bill Cosby, his tremendous appeal reaches both white and black audiences.

The raves from critics have continued.

After his second film, *Trading Places*, critic Richard Schnickel wrote: '[Murphy] . . . demonstrates the powers of invention that signal the arrival of a major comic actor and possibly a great star. He makes *Trading Places* something more than a good-hearted comedy. He turns it into an event.'

Newsweek: 'Murphy is the most dynamic new comic talent around, a quicksilver quick-change artist whose rapport with the audience is instantaneous.'

The moment he appeared on the screen in *Trading Places*, the audience broke out in whistles and cheers and began chanting 'Ed-die . . . Ed-die . . . '

'Ever hear an audience smile?' *Time* asked in 1983.

New York Times' Vincent Canby is as tough as they come. He stated: 'A terrific career is in store.'

Ralph Bellamy, one of the co-stars in *Trading Places*, commented, 'He listens and reacts before he speaks. You can see the brain working. It's an innate thing.'

Dan Aykroyd speaks quite often about Eddie, and every single comment is high praise.

'He's like a radar disc receiving signals, very raw and sensitive.'

Or, 'He has so much inbred talent – talent you can't teach, like the dexterity of the fingers of Barney Clark's surgeons. Talent like that is a very big shield.'

Saturday Night Live producer Dick Ebersol commented, 'The sky is the limit for Eddie Murphy!'

His directors join the chorus of praisers.

Walter Hill (he directed *48 Hrs.*): 'This kid is so enormously talented he can get away with anything.'

John Landis (director of *Trading Places*): 'Eddie is too smart not to realise how good he is.' Another time, Landis said, 'Eddie's effect was dazzling. There was a *ding!* when he walked on [the soundstage], almost like Marilyn Monroe.'

Eddie's *Beverly Hills Cop* director Martin Brest is the one who coined the phrase 'beyond brilliance' to describe his star.

He went on to say, 'He is a genius. I don't mean it like, "Hey, you're a genius, baby." I mean he's like nobody else around. It's spooky. He's so young. You wonder where he had time to pick up all this stuff.'

Brest also calls Eddie 'God's gift to a director, a high-performance, acting-comedy machine.'

In a *TV Guide* interview in 1982, it was reported that Eddie Murphy said that he felt he was destined for greatness (shades of Muhammad Ali?) a *Los Angeles Times* writer felt that he thereby 'put a monkey on the back of his talent,' and set up an additional tension in the mind of the audience.

But Eddie has kept proving what he said then, not the least in the hugely successful *Beverly Hills Cop* about which film the critics agree that it is definitely Eddie Murphy's movie, showing his wit, his intelligence, his razor-sharp comedic talent for all to see.

This may be the place to reiterate what we have heard before, but what actors, writers, and directors keep emphasising: Tragedy and drama are not easy, but comedy is the most difficult of all.

This is not a recent discovery. There was a great Shakespearian actor in the last century by the name of Edmund Keene, and he is reported to have uttered these words on his death bed: 'Dying is easy; comedy is hard.'

Eddie Murphy makes the stuff he does look easy as pie, and that may be the hardest and most admirable of all.

CATCH A COP

Eddie Murphy, star of Paramount's
runaway hit, *Beverly Hills Cop*,
has been chosen *Star of the Year*
for ShoWest '85.*
(Daily Variety)

*ShoWest is the association of exhibitors
in the twelve western states*

    Beverly Hills Cop is Eddie Murphy's fourth movie,
though he – and many of us – would like to call it his
third, quickly subtracting and forgetting number three,
Best Defence with Dudley Moore. That film was a total
flop, a dismal failure. Furthermore, it misled audiences
who came to see Eddie Murphy act with Dudley Moore,
an intriguing combination. What people got was a poor
film with Eddie in a non-funny cameo part, a
meaningless role.
    But *Beverly Hills Cop* has made up for it. It continues
to break box-office records.
    In the first twenty-three days of its release, this action
comedy grossed 64 million dollars. In the first thirty-four

days of release, it generated 100 million dollars at the box office.

In its first ten weeks of release, the film has made more than 150 million dollars.

And so it goes . . . on and on . . .

'Eddie Murphy?' said one exhibitor. 'That's a synonym for M-O-N-E-Y right now.'

A colleague of his interrupted. 'Right now? Listen, this is nothing but a preview of bigger things to come!'

By the way, talking to several real life Beverly Hills Cops – it seems that a goodly number of them have seen the film – they will, of course, disclaim any connection with reality, but they enjoy the movie thoroughly. He made the Beverly Hills cops laugh heartily.

Beverly Hills Cop is a Paramount film, part of the contract that the studio signed with Murphy in the summer of 1983, a contract that is a rarity. An exclusive, six-film, estimated 25 million dollar contract . . . As they say in Hollywood, 'There hasn't been a contract like this since the days of Marilyn Monroe!'

The contract also means that Eddie Murphy gets an undisclosed but substantial percentage of the distributor's *gross* on each film. Note: Yes, that's a percentage of the *gross*, not the more common percentage of net profit. Eddie Murphy gets a percentage of what his movies take in *before* all the expenses are paid. Few performers are anywhere near this position. Superstars such as Burt Reynolds and Clint Eastwood, possibly, and occasionally Robert Redford and Paul Newman, so far as one can guess. (The actual details of contracts are kept as secret as possible in a town where there are no real secrets).

No question about it: Since money is one way of measuring success, i.e. how many are willing to pay to see a specific artist, Eddie Murphy is unquestionably the hottest performer today!

In *Beverly Hills Cop*, Eddie plays his first *solo* starring role. In *48 Hrs*, he shared the honours with Nick Nolte, in *Trading Places* with Dan Aykroyd, and in *Best Defence* . . . well, let's forget *Best Defence*.

His portrait of the street-smart Detroit police detective who goes to fancy Beverly Hills to track down his best friend's killer is the work of a virtuoso.

It may be amusing to recall that the story was first intended for Mickey Rourke and, at one version of the screenplay, for Sylvester Stallone. This also indicates that the character did not have to be black. He is just a character who miraculously brings pomp and authority to its knees at every possible opportunity. The movie is a strange blend of violence and comedy, a dangerous mixture. Most feel that it is to a great extent thanks to Eddie Murphy that it does work. But work it does. People see it and they come out of the theatre loving Eddie Murphy. Which is why a movie that cost 14.8 million dollars to make is rapidly becoming one of the big money-makers in Hollywood history.

Everybody involved with the film sees Eddie as a comic actor with just about limitless potential.

'This guy will just go on and on,' is an often-heard comment from his colleagues, and that includes police inspector Gilbert Hill, who plays inspector Todd in the movie. Yes, the reel-life inspector is a real-life inspector – he has been with the Detroit Police Department since 1959, that department's top homicide cop. He showed the filmmakers around the police department, and they were so impressed with him that they signed him for his acting debut.

One of the film's fine actors is Judge Reinhold, who plays detective Rosewood, a nice and naive Beverly Hills cop. He has this to say about Eddie: 'I kept looking for his tragic flaw, but I couldn't find it. He's gifted, a comedic Mozart.'

Eddie Murphy, the actor, blends with Eddie Murphy, the writer.

Both the director, Martin Brest, and the screenwriter,

Daniel Petrie, Jr., give Eddie credit for several important script changes that endowed routine scenes with special and crazy magic.

Petrie points to the opening scene.

In this scene, the character Murphy plays (his name is Axel Foley) works undercover in order to bust a cigarette-smuggling ring in Detroit. He does a lengthy and rapid parody of street jive that's totally hilarious.

'You couldn't write down all the dialogue Eddie can use in one scene,' Petrie states. 'You'd have ten page scenes.'

Brest likes to talk about the scene where the character Foley bluffs his way into an exclusive men's club where the bad guy, the one with the deadly charm, Victor Maitland (played by Steven Berkoff), is dining with his matchingly wicked assistant (Jonathan Banks).

Early the very morning the scene was due to be shot, Brest walked over to Murphy's trailer to explain and discuss the problem he had with the scene. He had already considered and dismissed at least half a dozen versions of that scene. He was stuck.

'Eddie was still rubbing sleep from his eyes,' Brest says.

Eddie listened politely to the director. Then he sat and thought for a while. A short while.

Suddenly, he looked up and grinned.

He assumed the total character of a lisping, mincing and prancing caricature of a gay guy who gets past the maitre d' by giving an embarrassing account of herpes that must be conveyed to Maitland.

'It couldn't have taken him more than four seconds, but he proceeded to spill out the whole scene,' Brest marvels. 'I literally fell on the floor laughing. I couldn't stop laughing. Eddie put his makeup on, we walked over to the set, and he did it. Exactly like that. I think it's one of the funniest scenes in the movie.'

In Hollywood, people keep speculating about the

specific reasons for the fantastic and ongoing success of the film. It's a phenomenon, all agree. But nobody can tell exactly *why* the movie keeps bringing in astronomical sums at the box office. (There is speculation that it could gross more than 200 million dollars before the end of 1985 and possibly even surpass the all-time movie grosser, *E.T.*)

Most will agree that the main reason has to be – Eddie Murphy, giving a special life to the evasive, wise-cracking cop with a lot of street savvy as he keeps fighting against bureaucratic rules and regulations.

'I think it is very entertaining,' Murphy told *Jet* Magazine. 'It's not the answer to the cinema question, but this is the best one yet, as far as my acting goes.'

An executive at Paramount reveals that the project had been percolating at the studio for eight years without getting off the ground.

He also says that there is serious talk about a sequel to the film, and that a planned concert film is referred to on the lot as 'Beverly Hills Cop Goes to London.'

Eddie himself lets a pleased grin spread all over that handsome face with the dimple, happily admitting that he is delighted with the response to *Beverly Hills Cop*.

'You see, I had to make it funny. The film is my apology to the nation for *Best Defence*.'

DIG DEEPER

Who can wipe out joy?
Men have tried, in every age.
But they have not succeeded.
—*Henry Miller*

Where does it come from, the gift to perceive and to create anew? Or to give a glow of humour even to an ordinary event? To see the wonderful craziness all around, to make us laugh, even at ourselves?

Dan Aykroyd thinks it has to do with genetics.

'There are great surgeons who come out of the womb with great manual dexterity. From what I understand, Eddie's father was a funny guy. That's part of it. Some guys are just born to be race-car drivers; Eddie was born with a comic whim.'

Is it possible that it all began before birth? Was he letting out a giggle already in the womb? ('What *is* this place?!')

Certainly, the gift was there at an early age. He himself recalls childhood memories.

'My mother says I never talked in my own voice – always cartoon characters. Dudley Do-Right, Bullwinkle.

I used to do Sylvester the Cat ('thufferin' thuccotash') all the time. I could always get my brother Charlie mad by doing Bela Lugosi. Get him in trouble. I was that kind of kid.'

As is the case with many, if not most, creative individuals, he has an extraordinary memory for the absurdities and misunderstandings of childhood. He really remembers how it *felt*. He does a great impersonation of kids wanting ice cream. Of kids teasing each other. 'You can't get any ice cream . . . you're on welfare . . . Your father is an alcoholic . . . '

It all began early.

Both his parents worked (his stepfather as a foreman in an ice cream plant, his mother for the phone company), so it happened that young Eddie simply skipped school, stayed home and enjoyed himself in his own special way. He could put on Elvis Presley's 'Live at Madison Square Garden' album, dress up in a gold lamé coat an uncle had given him and go on swaggering and gyrating like Elvis until he dripped sweat.

'Elvis was my idol then. Still is,' he says. 'I thought he had more presence and charisma than anybody who ever existed.'

This does not stop him from doing heavy parodies of Elvis, butt sticking out, breaking wind . . .

Elvis and the gold lamé coat will make him recall one of life's embarrassing moments. One time his brother Charlie caught him in the act and watched him for quite a while before letting him know he was there.

'He said, "You're crazy, man. Really crazy." He wanted to know what I was rehearsing for. I had no answer.'

Not consciously at that time, but somewhere inside he must have known nearly always where he was going. The writer Ray Bradbury talks about a 'gyroscope in the blood,' something that pulls us toward a certain direction in life, draws us the way we are supposed to go. Eddie seems to exemplify this theory.

23

He is an intuitive comic, it has been said. What does it mean? That he knows without having learned? Does he have a seventh sense, the comic sense?

How does he go about it?

He began by looking at television. He still watches television and movies frequently. Does he compare that world with life as he discovers it bit by bit all around him?

Evidently, he is endlessly bemused by people and their reactions and activities. He watches all the time. He 'drains' people and takes them into himself, and then he shows us what he has seen.

He has an ear for the exact way people talk. He does replace dialogue in his films – he did that already in *48 Hrs*. Writers often present standard black dialogue while Eddie knows precisely how it ought to sound.

It is amazing when one considers that he is truly a child of the television age. His main experience, the bulk of his knowledge comes from that small screen. Somehow, he has learned to use that experience. Television has not used him, not dulled his senses and reduced his outlook to the two-dimensional level.

His eyes give him away. Look at his eyes! Really look at them.

They have not taken on the grey, neutral, electronic look of the tube. His eyes are not the cool, dead eyes of television, the *cold* medium. His eyes are filled with soul, with a kinship with everyone and everything that lives and breathes. Laughter is dancing in those big brown eyes. They are alive! They see!

When he is on the other side of the screen, that is when he performs on television, he has this unique, almost uncanny ability to talk right into the camera so that he seems to reach out and touch people watching in their homes. He removes some kind of barrier. He is not in any way intimidated by the camera. He talks to it as if to a person, a person to whom he can rap about anything.

The camera is his plaything, his tool . . . his utterly relaxed attitude is indeed remarkable.

He spouts four-letter words and what could be insults, but his eyes erase any misunderstandings.

His warmth comes through on the screen, and it is there, a tangible reality, when one meets him in person.

'He is kind, a real gentleman, he respects people around him,' say crew members (and from those one hears the real truth about a performer). He behaves as if he lives in the natural climate of the human family.

He seems strangely free of fear, hate, jealousy, doubt, and suspicion . . . as if he has reached – or been born with – a harmony between his inner and outer worlds.

This is why he gets away with the outrageous things he keeps getting away with. He has a 'dirty mouth' ('my humour is *mean*, man!'), but his sense of the comical has not diffracted into bitterness, envy or malice.

Eddie Murphy, a mischievous but favourite child of America, of mankind . . .

EVER ELEGANT

Too much of a good thing
can be wonderful.
—*Mae West*

'Eddie loves clothes, jewellery, cars and women – but not necessarily in that order,' says Eddie Murphy's manager, Robert Wachs.

Imagine that, a stand-up comic with sex appeal! He has a lithe body, almost five-foot-ten, and weighs between 155 and 160 pounds.

He moves beautifully, like an athlete or a young, healthy animal.

'Girls think I am handsome because I act handsome,' claims he.

He is a bit vain. It was a fact, even as a child, his mother says. 'He looks in that mirror, and he's on a natural high.' He always liked to adorn himself with accessories. He habitually spent a lot of time combing his hair except for one year (in fifth grade) when he didn't comb it all for the whole year, and his friends nicknamed him 'Peas.'

He likes jewellery, mainly chains and rings and mostly

in gold. Often he wears a gold medallion with the letters EM set in light-catching diamonds.

He's heavily into leather. Often black leather: Leather pants, leather cap, leather jacket with no shirt!

Now, let it be said, once and for all: Some men have it, and some men don't. We are talking about the ability to wear a leather jacket and *no shirt under it*.

Prince can do it. Richard Gere can do it. Eddie Murphy certainly can do it. But few, very few other men can.

He also wears a T-shirt well, as was evident in *Beverly Hills Cop* where he wore one for the whole film. That was a Mumford High School physical education department T-shirt (the film's producer, Jerry Brukheimer, is a 1961 Mumford graduate). The school has been deluged with orders for the T-shirts from all over. The cost is ten dollars, and the sale of them has brought the school welcome money for student activities.

There are also fake Mumford T-shirts on the market, we hear, but they tend to sell for more.

Oh yes, *People Magazine* labelled Eddie Murphy as one of this country's best dressed men.

Some people prefer him in black leather, some scream with delight when he dons a white-on-white leather outfit, and some love a red leather unzipped to the waist . . . or a black-sequined jacket open half-way to the waist. Echoes of Elvis Presley when Elvis was young and gorgeous . . .

On the much-talked about HBO special, he wore tight red leather, showing a lot of chest and wearing a loose hip belt with a goldtipped end that snapped in happy rhythms against his genitals as he moved swiftly across that stage.

He looks terrific in a tuxedo (red bow-tie) and privately he may relax in a blue or white Nike jogging suit or in a kimono-like robe.

His co-manager Richard Tienken said, 'He's the only comedian who dresses like a rock star.'

Somebody else (when talking about drugs and living in the fast line) commented, 'Not Eddie. No chance. Not ever. He's too vain to destroy himself.'

His clothes are not inexpensive – if he sees a leather jacket for four hundred or five hundred dollars and wants it, he just buys it. Money problems are not his anymore. He is a millionaire, and he dresses like one, on his own terms.

He buys expensive shoes also, often Italian, often Gucci.

A favourite story about him goes something like this. He was on his way to an appointment in an office building. As he exited the car, he happened to step right into a pile of dog shit on the sidewalk outside.

He looked down, hardly lost a beat, and stepped right out of the shoes, leaving them sitting there on the concrete as a monument to being rich and cool.

'He's got style,' said someone admiringly. Well, why not, if you can afford such gestures for a laugh.

FAMILY FOUNDATION

The people who see miracles are
the people who look for miracles,
the people who open their eyes to
the miracles that surround us always.
—*Tom Robbins*

We hear about divorces, child abuse, sibling rivalry
. . . generation gaps and misunderstandings and unwilling-
ness to communicate or inability to relate. The world is
filled with desperately lonely people, tremendously
insecure people, people who lead lives of 'quiet desper-
ation,' uncertain if they can cope.

Reading the newspapers and hearing TV news, one
may come to accept this as a normal, meaning most
common, condition.

What is the miracle that could cure our ills, make us
whole again and glad to be alive?

It has to be love. The real love that means understanding. The wisdom of the heart.

The author Henry Miller calls love the 'be-all, end-all,
and cure-all.'

And what does Eddie Murphy have to say about it?

He says very directly, 'Man, when you've been loved a lot, you're not afraid. People who haven't been loved a lot worry about what's going to happen to them.'

It all begins in the cradle, so to speak. To be surrounded by love, to get into the habit of love, to feel worthy of being loved, to feel like *someone* . . . that's greatly dependent on what takes place during early childhood.

Eddie Murphy has always known love.

'My foundation . . . the truth,' are the words he uses to describe his family and his relationship to the members of it.

Family is his centre.

Eddie was born in the Bushwick section of Brooklyn on April 3, 1961, the second son of Charles Murphy, a city transit policeman, and his wife Lillian, a telephone operator.

When Eddie was three, his parents divorced, and six years later, Lillian married Vernon Lynch, a trim, soft-spoken, hard-working man.

Lynch was once a professional boxer, featherweight. He kept working as a part-time boxing coach while he supported his family by his job as foreman at Breyers Ice Cream Plant. Lillian also kept working for the telephone company. Both of them had ambitions to make things better, to keep moving upward.

Vernon Lynch took his position as stepfather to the two boys, Charles and Eddie, seriously. He and Lillian had another son, Vernon.

When Eddie was ten, the family moved to the primarily black, middle- and lower-class Long Island suburb of Roosevelt, twenty miles from Manhattan.

Eddie's biological father had died a couple of years earlier, stabbed by his girlfriend during an argument.

'A victim of the Murphy charm,' Eddie may comment about this, the only real tragedy in his life.

There was a brief but bad time in his early childhood. Shortly after the parents had separated, Lillian took ill and had to be hospitalised. Charlie and Eddie were placed with a foster mother for a while. 'She was bad, man,' he recalls. 'Those were bad days,' he says, speaking of his foster mother. 'And bad, bad, bad food. She's the reason I have a warped sense of humour.'

Lillian recovered, however, and the family was reunited.

Eddie has little memory of his actual father, but his mother says that Eddie is much like him. 'A very charming man. Very charming. He'd sing and tell jokes . . . and two of Eddie's uncles are still part-time comics.' The genetic factor?

Now, when Eddie talks about Vernon Lynch, he talks about him as his father because that is what he has been and is.

Both parents say that Eddie was not a problem kid and did not need a lot of discipline. Except that he hated to do his part of the household chores.

'You better become famous or rich, boy, for you're the laziest kid I've seen,' Lynch used to say.

Mother Lillian covered up at times, but she admits, 'He was never into manual labour, I guess . . . He washed his hands a lot. He didn't like to take out the garbage at all . . .'

Yes, Vernon was a loving man, but he was also something of a taskmaster. He made sure his family had what they needed ('we always wanted to go forward . . . Eddie didn't ever know about the ghetto,' he points out with deserved pride), but he wanted to make sure that the boys learned responsibility, too. And he did not want any weaklings for sons.

Regularly, he would make them put on boxing gloves and go a few rounds with him in the basement.

He says that Eddie could have been a fighter, especially because of his sure timing, except he 'never liked to get hit. He didn't like to act tough. He preferred to act silly.'

'He always had a special sweetness about him,' his

mother says. 'And he understood things . . . it was uncanny sometimes how a little kid could understand so much. He'd look at me with those big eyes and say, It's okay, Mommy, I know you get mad and spank me because you love me. If you didn't care, you wouldn't . . . '

Eddie's very earliest ambition was to own a Mister Softee truck and get free ice cream, all he wanted. That ambition, however, was soon pushed out of his mind by another one, a bigger one. An ambition that filled his head every waking hour and would let nothing stop him.

Mother Lillian was determined, for her part, that Eddie should go to college. But school didn't interest him, except as a place where he found a captive audience.

Actually, he did enroll in college, Nassau Community College, in the fall of 1980, but his college career lasted only weeks since fate (and the producers of 'Saturday Night Live') had another thing in store . . .

Neither his parents nor relatives and family friends considered doing comedy acts a real, honest job. 'I tried to discourage him,' his mother admits. 'But that's all he wanted to do . . . '

The parents worried about his laziness and wanted him to get up in the morning and do something real. Eddie did what they wanted. He got up in the morning, went out . . . and straight to a friend's house to catch some sleep because he worked late hours in small clubs all over.

When Eddie was seventeen, his mother came to hear his routine. Afterwards, she asked him where he'd learned to talk so dirty! (To this day, Eddie keeps a cleaner language around his parents and grandparents than around anyone else.)

His parents have, of course, heard him many times since then. His mother beams with pride ('I'm glad I didn't manage to stop him!') but is also careful to warn friends that his live performances are not suitable for children.

Sometimes his stepfather seems a little stunned at Eddie's enormous success, and who wouldn't be? Thinking back, he reflects, 'He always did believe in himself. Even when he was a little kid. That kind of confidence could have made him a dynamite middle-weight boxer. And those reflexes . . . they are good. More than good. Oh well . . . at least, he can defend himself. But he doesn't like to fight. Not that way.'

His mother goes back to Eddie's intensive watching of television. 'He was crazy about *West Side Story*. He saw it I don't know how many times,' she told a friend.

She believes his main influences were three things he watched all he could on television: *West Side Story*, Elvis Presley, and Bruce Lee.

But she must know that she was perhaps the greatest influence of them all.

Eddie's mother is a strong woman with a straight-forward way of speaking. She also has a lot of charm and an always-ready laughter in her eyes. Funny? Yes, she has a tremendous sense of humour, of the warm kind.

The family bonds remain very strong, in spite of Eddie's heavy joking about members of his family.

His stepfather will acknowledge that Eddie's parody of a drunk father may be built on an incident or two that actually took place. There is no explaining away in the family. Everybody does something crazy sometimes, and they accept that Eddie remembers it all and will use it as material. They also know that Eddie's love is there, and they accept him in a no-nonsense sort of way.

'Eddie really believes in family togetherness and he finds solace in the company of his family,' says his manager.

Eddie has a special relationship with his brothers Charlie and Vernon. He often brings his younger brother (actually half-brother) Vernon with him to California when he is filming, living in a rented hillside mansion, and his older brother Charlie works for him.

The brothers kid around a lot. Sure, the brothers admire Eddie, but they refuse flatly to treat him as some kind of star. 'That's my brother . . . I've seen his dirty underwear,' they may say.

Eddie becomes serious when he talks about his family.

'My family's happiness is *the* most important thing to me,' he says simply.

GAY GOADING

No two persons agree on the
definitions of the six deadly
adjectives: obscene, lewd,
lascivious, filthy, indecent,
disgusting.

What is funny, and what is offensive?

'It's outrageous. I would never go to see a movie or anything featuring Eddie Murphy.'

That is a gay man speaking. His sentiments are echoed by many others.

'Anti-gay bigotry.'

'Stereotypes.'

'Murphy's anti-gay bias is offensive.'

'It's just plain poor taste.'

'Filth and prejudices, that's all he has to offer.'

'It's ugly . . . Talk about hitting below the belt . . . '

One gay man is thoughtful. 'Sure. He goes too far. His Home Box Office special was a bit much. The AIDS jokes in particular. No, I wasn't really offended, but a bit shocked at his crudeness. He goes the limit . . . '

'Murphy is not a very sensitive man. I feel a little sorry for him.'

'Perhaps he doesn't realise that a homosexual's life is not always easy. His jokes don't make life any easier, and I resent that.'

'We all choose what we are. I have chosen to be gay, he has chosen to be insensitive. I'd rather be gay . . . '

'It's outrageous and insulting!'

'It's horrible. How would he feel if someone stood up and made fun of blacks and thereby fostered prejudices that we are fighting against?!'

Yes, many gays are boycotting Eddie Murphy products. 'Faggot jokes' and jokes about AIDS, the burlesque takeoff of 'The Honeymooners' about a pair of gay lovers ('The Homo-mooners'), coming to Hollywood and finding a gay Mr. T . . . these routines offend and disgust some.

After his HBO special in the latter part of 1983 (with many reruns), one group formed the Eddie Murphy's Disease Foundation – the disease being uncontrollable fear of homosexuality. (The group seems to have dissolved, however. Letters to the given address are returned.)

On that aforementioned HBO special, he spoke about having nightmares about gay people and mimicked being ordered to pleasure Mr. T. and playing tennis with gay people, but it was especially the joke about the very serious illness AIDS (Acquired Immune Deficiency Syndrome) that offended. 'Girls hang out with them [the gays], and one night they're having fun and they give them a little kiss and they go home with AIDS on their lips.'

In a *Rolling Stone* magazine interview, he speaks about his gay jokes. ' . . . I poke fun at everybody, 'cause I'm not a racist, I'm not a sexist; I'm just *out there*. I use racial slurs, but I don't hate anybody.'

He goes on to say (in the same interview): 'This is what I have to say about homosexuals. I'm not the first comic to do homosexual jokes. When I said I was afraid of homosexuals, all it was was a setup for my Mr. T. joke. I don't have anything against homosexuals, I'm not afraid of them. I know homosexuals. It was a *joke*. I make fun of *everybody*; I poke fun at anything that I think is funny. It's comedy. It's not real.'

He goes on to make a distinction between 'homosexuals' and 'faggots,' believing that the first group did not feel offended while the latter did.

Does he care that he has upset many people?

In some interviews, one gets a feeling that he doesn't.

But he does. When he's totally serious, he will stress that he cares. But he insists, 'I wasn't being malicious. I know in my heart that I don't hate gay people.'

In a frank and recent interview in *Parade* magazine, he offers a quite strong apology . . . an apology that has been mentioned in various news programmes.

He tells that some of the reactions after the HBO special did scare him. Then he found out that half the letters were bad, half were good. Then the recording of the same concert went gold, and then it won a Grammy . . .

'I'm only 23 years old,' he told the interviewer. 'And I'm growing into something else.'

Having said that God is the only one he would apologise to, he does go on to making an apology in these words:

'I want to apologise to the gay people – I've never really apologised. And to anyone else who's been offended by any kind of things I've done.'

He also makes amends to Lucille Ball, Red Skelton, Jackie Gleason and anyone else who has been offended by his act and his language.

He points out that he feels that the misunderstandings, so far as veteran comedians' disapproval, stem from a generation gap.

He was told that Lucille Ball (in a *TV Guide* article) stated her concern with the effect television has on children and called Murphy 'bright as all get out . . . and then he uses that kind of language. All I could think of was, "Why?" It's not going to hurt his career, but it hurt my feelings. With all his talent, why did he resort to that?'

Eddie took time to think.

Then he said, 'Lucy and Gleason are from the old school of comedy. In terms of Lucy being hurt, I understand. I don't expect a 70-year-old woman to be into my show. We have different values.'

But he is not defensive about his material. He will take criticism seriously. He will consider objections to aspects of his acts.

For now, he sent a 'big, wet kiss' to everyone.

'Sorry, I'm just trying to get a laugh. I'm not a hateful person. I get on stage because I like to see people laugh. I don't have to go on tour; I could just do movies. But I like to see people smile. I don't want to hurt them.'

And everyone is not hurt.

An elderly man who is gay, fat, and Jewish admitted that he finds Eddie uproariously funny.

'Perhaps I shouldn't. I mean, the joke about AIDS was a bit too much, but his other gay jokes make me laugh. He also makes fun of fat people, like when he talks about fat people needing designer jeans, too. He does a lot of Yiddish jokes – I admire this black guy who can top some Jewish comedians, both when it comes to accent and content . . . I just think the guy is funny. And you know, a wise man said that we don't really have a sense of humour if we can't laugh at ourselves. Eddie Murphy has helped me to laugh at myself and he has made my life better for it . . . '

HIGHER AND HIGHER

I know two kinds of audiences only—
one coughing and one not coughing.
—*Artur Schnabel*

In the case of Eddie Murphy, he knows that if he is not funny, the audience won't laugh. If people laugh, then he is doing something right.

It's a constant challenge, it's a balancing act. It is taking risks every time he goes out on that stage and meets an audience, face to face. Sometimes it works, and sometimes it doesn't.

Stand-up comedy is not for cowards. Imagine standing there, all alone in the bright lights for all to see, having no script but your own, no ideas but your own . . . Even riding the crest of popularity as he is – and nobody will argue with his superb ability as a comic actor – sometimes the result is a reaction that flatters, sometimes one that flattens.

Perhaps that is why he keeps doing it and plans to keep on doing it. The spring of 1985, as a matter of fact, he made another tour from place to place, from stage to stage.

He himself points out that a stand-up comic has to

keep doing what he is doing or he will get rusty, according to the rule, 'What you don't use, you lose.'

And he is a bit addicted to going out on that stage.

'Applause is like medicine. I just walk into a club and people start clapping. I feel like saying, Thanks, I was really depressed, but I'm not now, so I'm leaving.'

A change is slowly seeping into his material.

He is very young, and he keeps growing up right in front of our eyes.

'It used to be that just saying an obscenity was funny. Now, I work with more material.'

He has, for instance, taken on Jerry Falwell and the Moral Majority: 'I'll put the majority of my foot up your moral butt.'

He is definitely a Movie Star now. What are his ambitions at this point in time?

He doesn't go around talking too much about them except to say, 'I have so much I want to do in this business.'

When pressed further, he may admit that he wants to direct and write and score and produce movies.

'Like Chaplin used to do. Nobody does that anymore.'

Chaplin, no less! Chaplin . . . that genius of comedy, that great little man . . .

Evidently, he is considering a remake of Charlie Chaplin's movie *The Kid*, which was made in 1921 with Jackie Coogan as an orphan, raised in the streets by Chaplin. The two of them live on their wits. The kid breaks windows, Chaplin repairs them. Then the child takes ill, and Chaplin must bring him to the hospital. The authorities try to take the child away from him then. It is not his child, after all, and he is not a suitable person to raise a child.

That movie awakened some special emotions inside Eddie Murphy, and the idea of him doing a remake is intriguing. It would give him a chance to show gentler sides of his humour. So far, so much of it has appeared

40

along with street-tough guy aspects, with violence, with four-letter words . . .

But don't talk to him about making 'arty' movies – all he wants is to make truly entertaining movies.

'I don't want Oscars, I just want the audience to enjoy my movies. Like, Clint Eastwood doesn't win Oscars, but he's the biggest star in the world. The hell with all that other stuff.'

Not a bad attitude. Entertain, make good entertaining movies, and let art happen if it happens . . . the accident of art, as it were.

Will he pull other black people with him as he keeps going up? Does he feel any kind of 'racial responsibility?'

Yes, he does.

He feels that he has a certain responsibility to push some doors open, to smooth a couple of rough spots, to help other talented blacks get a foot into the entertainment field.

'But I don't think I ought to alienate competent white people to do it. I'm not going to have a racist production company. But I'm real too. I am not going to lie. If a black guy and a white guy have exactly the same credentials and I like them both the same, I'd probably hire the black guy. But competence is competence. That's what it's about.'

Movie manuscripts are delivered by the truckload to the Eddie Murphy Productions in New York. It is not difficult for anyone to figure out that if you get Eddie Murphy to make your movie, you have it made. He is the one who decides what he will do next. A check with his company gives no definite answers. Only a general statement that he is considering several possibilities.

There has been talk of him doing the Jackie Wilson movie . . . or doing a 'buddy movie' with his close friend Joe Piscopo (who is making the movie 'Wise Guys' with Danny De Vito for Brian De Palma – yes, *that* De Palma and yes, it's a comedy) . . .

41

There has been talk of him making a film with Drew Barrymore . . . and of one teaming him with Robin Williams. He once said to Vanessa Williams (the short-lived Miss America) that he would make a film with her.

He would like to make a film with the two he admires tremendously, Richard Pryor and Bill Cosby. He and Pryor have discussed some more definite ideas.

A spoof entitled, 'I'm Gonna Get You, Sucker,' has been discussed.

Just about every day, a new idea or several are presented to him. He will weigh one thing against another and wait for that click inside his head that is going to tell him that this particular story is just the one for him to go with.

There is also his music becoming increasingly important in his life. He is writing, composing, singing . . . and before long we will hear the result.

One thing is for sure: He will continue to appear in the four major media: TV, records, concerts, and movies.

His explanation as to why he wouldn't just give up the rest, his stand-ups and concerts, and concentrate on movies went like this:

'See, if I did just movies, I wouldn't be living on the east side of the country. I'd have to stay in Los Angeles then, and with the sexual freedom out there, you can catch stuff that'll make your thing fall off!'

The truth is that his energy and creativity demand various forms of expression.

One does not wonder that his managers do not manage anyone else and that they have absolutely no plans to manage anyone else. Eddie Murphy is enough!

'One thing,' he says thoughtfully. 'I've good vibes. I know when something's right. I'm going to trust my intuition. My feeling. Only once didn't I do it, and that was with *Best Defence*. It's the only time I've gone for just the money. Listen. They offered me more than I'd made for *48 Hrs.* and *Trading Places* together, and I fell for it. Never again . . . not unless it's a tremendously big cheque . . . ' He laughs.

One must agree with *Newsweek*: 'To waste as precious (and expensive) a commodity as Eddie Murphy on something as flat and unprofitable as last summer's *Best Defence* is like spreading caviar on stale Wonder Bread.'

He's going higher, and there won't be any more stale bread in his future, whatever money is offered . . . but there's going to be a lot of caviar!

INFLAMMATORY INFLUENCE?

Go out there. Amuse and
confuse and stir up things!
—*Henry Miller*

His Mr. Robinson is a ghetto-version of Mr. Rogers.
'Oh! Here's Mr. Landlord with an eviction notice . . . '
Smiling his wide smile right into the camera. 'Now, kids,
can you say, "Mutha"?'
Kids are invited to sing along with Mr. Robinson:
> 'It's one hell of a day in the neighbourhood
> A hell of a day for a neighbour.
> Would you be mine? Could you be mine?
> I'd love to move to your neighbourhood someday
> — Only trouble is, when I move in, y'all move away
> Let's have a drink, let's have a smoke,
> You bring the cash 'cause Robinson's broke
> Will you be, won't you be, my neighbour?'
His Tyrone Green, the menacing convict/writer (he
debuted in a skit called 'Prose and Cons' – and there are
those who see a likeness between him and the young and

44

angry Eldridge Cleaver), recites a poem entitled 'I Hate White People.' The finishing line goes like this: 'I hate white people because they is white – W-I-T-E.' His spelling prowess or lack of such is demonstrated in the poem he writes in prison (it wins the poetry contest):

'Kill my landlord.

Kill my landlord.

C-I-L-L my landlord.'

The same Tyrone Green entertained a veteran's organisation by singing,

'Kill the white people

Yeah, mon,

Kill de white people.'

Inflammatory?

Or the kind of humour that lets us look right through what we may avoid talking about in our polite encounters with each other or avoid thinking about in quiet moments . . . ? Letting us look right at it and through it, we may just come out on the other side feeling better!

Then there is his Stevie Wonder impersonation that usually upsets a few.

Eddie puts on sunglasses, lets his head wobble, and parodies the singer's smile, as he is delivering a rambling and endless acceptance speech at a Grammy Awards presentation.

He has been criticised for that one.

So what did he do?

He turned right around and incorporated some of the criticism he has received for this skit right into the routine.

He whipped off the dark glasses. 'Say, man, that ain't funny. He blind. Stevie be blind. Be sick to make fun of a blind man. What's wrong with you? Your mama raised you wrong!'

Unkind?

Stevie Wonder himself finds it hilarious.

As a matter of fact, the two of them met for the first

45

time in a club right after Eddie had done his Stevie impersonation.

And there was the time on *Saturday Night Live* when Eddie Murphy actually gave Stevie Wonder lessons in how to behave as Stevie Wonder!

'What can he do?' says Eddie with a grin. 'I could always *out box* him if I wanted to.'

'My experience is what I share with the audiences,' says Eddie Murphy. 'I don't look at them and say, Boy, aren't you funny. I'm looking at them, saying, My, aren't we all messed up! Like when I do a sketch like Buckwheat, I'm laughing at how ridiculous it was. Buckwheat was so absurd, it had to be parodied. Half the laughter is the absurdity of what I'm doing, and the other half is, Wow, the country's messed up! All about the good old days and the fifties and all that stuff – *Happy Days*, bull!'

In an interview when he was twenty-one, he went further into the subject of the television series *Happy Days* and what it represented on television.

'Black people, we didn't have no malt shop like Fonz. I'll tell you I am serious onstage when I talk about the reckless-eyeball charge. Used to be black man go to jail in Atlanta for "reckless eyeball," looking at a white woman. Happy Days! We got one hero – Martin Luther King. He's the only hero we have. And they killed him. We ain't been having no happy days.'

He touches on touchy subjects, as when he claims to have received jokes from President Reagan himself, such as:

'There are three things a black can't get: a black eye, a fat lip, and a job . . . '

Upsetting? Inflammatory?

Does he mean to be inflammatory? Does he want to jolt his audiences?

He laughs. He shrugs.

'I want a laugh . . . '

More seriously, 'I don't know exactly what I want to say . . . I want to be different.'

And different may mean telling it as he sees it and throwing some punches that may sting.

Perhaps his colleague Judge Reinhold (from *Beverly Hills Cop*) hit the nail on the head when he said, 'He's the Muhammad Ali of comedy.'

Reinhold also said, 'I love that guy. I absolutely love that guy.'

JOKES AND JIVING

Right now, I'm gonna have fun.
—*Eddie Murphy*

At the tender age of fifteen, Eddie Murphy's life changed.

He was already known for his quick repartees. So was a friend of his, Mickael Kyser (who also became a stand-up comic). Consequently, the two of them were asked to be hosts of talent shows at the youth centre where they hung out.

It was during such a talent show that it happened. A shiver of determination went up Eddie's spine. He looked around the room and then went over to the record player. He put on a record with Al Green singing. Eddie himself sang along, moving and gyrating a la Elvis, the way he had practised at home when playing hooky from school.

'Girls started screaming, and I said, Shit, you can't make girls scream doing a lot of other jobs, such as driving an ice cream truck.'

He and Kyser formed a band, but their repertoire was so limited that Eddie began to tell jokes between songs to make the act longer.

That was it.

He became obsessed.

He performed whenever he could. The Roosevelt High School auditorium, local bars, youth centres . . .

At one time, he teamed up with two white would-be-comedians, Rob Bartlett and Bob Nelson. They called themselves The Identical Triplets. Their biggest number was the 'reverse Oreo cookie' . . . That's right, Eddie stood between the other two . . . All three also did skits as elderly Jewish gentlemen, and Eddie's accent is still just about perfect.

Before long, Eddie was doing stand-up acts for which he got paid, making between twenty-five and fifty dollars a week, appearing in 'Gong Shows' (often taking home the twenty-five dollar prize), performing in Long Island nightclubs where he was still too young to enter as a customer.

At sixteen, he was beginning to feel like a star. After all, he did get money for some of his appearances. He began to wear an ascot and jacket and carry a brief-case.

He appeared at the White House Inn in Massapequa, Long Island, at Mr. Micks in Hempstead, the Blue Dolphin in Uniondale, My Father's Place in Roslyn . . .

'Didn't have much ghetto experience to draw on so I did impressions.'

He did, for instance, Robert Blake as Baretta, Bruce Lee, Howard Cosell, and Bill Cosby.

Mainly though, his act was a tribute to Richard Pryor, meaning that he used material he lifted directly from Pryor albums.

'Pryor isn't my biggest influence, he's my only influence,' he said at one time. 'I have all the admiration and respect in the world for that dude. He got status and respect just by being his own outrageous self, on his own terms.'

'If you heard me at eighteen, it was the Richard

49

experience. I was phrasing like Richard, talking like Richard, doing the same kind of jokes. As I get older, I don't get so hung up on that idol stuff. I become more and more myself.'

Armed with that unique self-assurance of his, Eddie Murphy walked into the Comic Strip in 1979, just months out of high school. (Yes, he graduated, through with some difficulty. He had to make up classes during the summer. His grade average? A weak C.)

The Comic Strip is a club on Manhattan's East Side, owned by Bob Wachs and Richie Tienken. Today, they are his managers!

But that first time they saw him, he was so impatient to show his stuff that he tried to bluff his way onstage right away, refusing to wait his turn.

Wachs, who was in charge, sent him packing. But the following week, there he was again.

'His material wasn't out of this world,' Wachs recalls. 'But he had great presence.'

The routine they heard, spiced with a lot of the vocabulary and machismo of urban street talk, was, of course, borrowed heavily from Richard Pryor.

Anyhow, Eddie got a job which led to more club dates up and down the East Coast.

Not only that, Wachs and Tienken offered to manage him.

Tienken was the owner of the Comic Strip, and Wachs is a lawyer who used to specialise in tax shelter investments. He admits that Eddie's career has become a passion to him.

'I dropped almost everything in my life to do this. I developed tunnel vision when it came to Eddie Murphy. Nobody his age has created this much excitement since I don't know when. I knew what he was and what he was capable of. I, moreover, have the energy, the knowledge, the wherewithal, and, quite modestly, the brains to pull it off.'

Wachs heard that *Saturday Night Live* needed another performer and that black would be just beautiful at that particular moment in time.

In the beginning, Eddie Murphy just got a piece on the show now and then.

Initially, he was considered the replacement for Garrett Morris, the only black performer from the old *Saturday Night Live*, but Murphy quickly grew beyond that and became the most popular performer on the late-night programme, writing all of his own material.

For this show, the programme is blocked out by segments, indicating various acts. But for Eddie, it just said, 'Eddie.' Meaning he could do whatever he wanted to with his spots.

All this happened after that time when the show ran four minutes short, and Eddie got the chance to go in and just fill those minutes. During that short period, a television star was born.

What did he do?

Well, he had night club material, but that was material spiced with four- and twelve-letter words. You can't say those words on television. So he had to go in, do routines, and quickly *remove* any 'offensive' word. He had to edit his own material right there, as he delivered it, with the television camera picking up every movement and every syllable, and millions of viewers watching.

What he did was nothing less than brilliant and remarkable, so say all who were present.

There was never jealousy on the part of the other performers in *Saturday Night Live*. Eddie's talent and genuine warmth took care of that.

He kept *Saturday Night Live* exactly that – alive – almost singlehandledly after the original cast had abandoned the show.

The following (second) season he was signed on as a regular, and for four seasons, he had the SNL audience (on some nights it reached twenty million viewers!) in stitches as he kept stretching his talent, inventing new characters, slashing at everyone and everything.

When Eddie was twenty, the supervising producer of the show exclaimed, 'I can't believe he's only twenty years old, he's so self-assured. He's the youngest person in the cast, yet he's got by far the strongest sense of his own style. He looks great. The camera loves him.'

Over and over, his colleagues point out that he has a definite love affair with the camera – and it seems to be a love without fear.

He must have been born fearless with extra helpings of self-assurance and confidence. For instance, in the beginning as well as now, he seldom rehearses his stage act. All the material is his own. Some of his best writing is totally improvised on the spot in the spotlight.

He likes it that way. He wants to keep a touch of the spontaneous, the improvised, even a miniscule hesitance which you have to look hard to notice.

'Audiences can tell if you are *too* confident,' he points out. 'They like a little vulnerability. They like to think they'd really like you if they got to know you.'

Chances are they would . . .

KICKS AND KINSHIP

You cheat yourself by
getting high . . .
—*Eddie Murphy*

Naturally, your surroundings shape your sense of humour. Though Eddie Murphy did not come from the ghetto, he grew up surrounded by tough kids, ready to tease him about anything that was different.

'In a tough neighbourhood – and almost any neighbourhood is tough in one way or another to a kid – you either conform or you are funny,' says a friend of his. 'And not little scared funny, but real, hilarious, irresistibly funny.'

Not only was he funny, but he was so sure of where he was going that he did not even try to be funny all the time. (Still doesn't.) He knew where he was going, what he wanted, and school wasn't it. He took his lessons elsewhere – in front of the TV, in a park, wherever there were human beings. Once he came to class totally unprepared, and when the teacher upbraided him, he boasted that he was going to become bigger than Bob Hope. The response? Well, he was forced to repeat the tenth grade.

This was tough for his ego. 'As vain as I was, I don't have to tell you what that did to me.'

He went to summer school, to night school, doubled up on classes and graduated only a couple of months late.

But school was just not his thing.

'I was articulate, with a strong vocabulary, but most of the courses bored me. I mean E equals mc squared . . . who gives a damn! My focus was my comedy. You could usually find me in the lunchroom trying out my routines on the kids to perform them in clubs later that night.'

Actually, that began in the third grade, when a teacher told the class that whoever made up the best story would win an Eskimo Pie.

Who do you think won it? That's right. Eddie received his first award then with a story about rice and Orientals. Nobody could stop him after that!

The kids around him responded to him. He was voted the most popular boy in his class.

In the senior yearbook, he turned serious and wrote: 'All men are sculptors, constantly chipping away the unwanted parts of their lives, trying to create their idea of a masterpiece.'

He also wrote under Future Plans: 'Comedian.'

Just like that.

Because his idea of a masterpiece had to do with humour, and the ones he felt the greatest kinship with were Richard Pryor and Bill Cosby. He commented once, 'There is nothing wrong with aspiring to be like someone you really admire; it's a great way to learn.'

The kinship is indeed still there, but Eddie is different, not the least from Pryor. Pryor's comedy seems to grow out of deep-seated conflict and pain, while Murphy is more of the naughty child. There is a naughtiness about him that makes you feel warm all over.

'He doesn't play the underdog. He is, as one writer put it, 'a hot dog, full of sass and guileless assurance.'

Eddie himself has said, 'Richard is funny as the victim, but I'm funnier when I try to fight back. Maybe the star of the 90's will be the funny black guy who runs the show. It would be nice to see that progression.'

Newsweek pointed out that *the terror behind the swagger* is a fundamental of Richard Pryor's appeal. Behind Eddie Murphy's posture of confidence, however, is – deeper confidence.

Another difference is that Eddie does not go the way of drugs. He doesn't touch drugs. Never has. (And Richard Pryor doesn't either, not anymore.)

'You cheat yourself by getting high, because you're running from a lesson you're being taught. I want to have all the hurts I'm supposed to have in my life, because that's where the comedy comes from.'

Parade magazine featured an interview with Eddie Murphy which to a great extent treated the subject: Why Eddie Murphy Won't Do Drugs.

He says that his parents lectured him about drugs and the dangers, but he did not need their warnings.

'When a person finds out I don't do drugs, that makes me seem hipper. Hip is being the one that goes, "Nah, I don't need that – I don't need a crutch." '

He has noticed that people on drugs increase their problems, both in number and magnitude. Those on depressants can't deal with what comes up in life. Others are on stimulants, and they lose their judgment.

Neither appeals to him.

He doesn't feel overly sympathetic towards celebrities who use drugs. He himself has climbed up from lower middle class, has overcome lack of a higher education – he has made it without resorting to drugs to relieve the pressures. He feels that everybody has pressures to cope with, not just celebrities. Also that using drugs or not using drugs is a matter of will . . . perhaps the will to really live life, face reality, without being either doped up and half asleep or falsely elated.

55

As a rule, he doesn't preach about drugs.

'I don't think that entertainers should be heroes, or preachers. If people want to imitate my drug-free life, fine. But I'm not trying to make any statements with it.'

Naturally, he knows people who are on drugs, and he lets them be.

'It's just that I find no need to be high. I have nothing to run from.'

What gives him his kicks?

Mainly work, his kind of work. The magic of it holds him in its grip. He cannot quite explain how it happens, how he creates his material.

'All my stuff comes to me totally spontaneously. I mean, like fully worked-out sketches pop into my head all laid out.'

He did get a kick out of a trip to Paris recently where he met the press of Europe. He also went to the fancy Crazy Horse Club feasting his eyes on the beautiful dancing girls. He stayed at Hotel Crillon and found that he could, by golly, make even the French laugh.

'Should learn French, though. That would be a kick. I mean, I could say what I say now, but it would sound *elegant!* Like in "I smell merde" . . . '

One of his big, big kicks happened in 1983.

Richard Pryor had been on the Johnny Carson show and the talk slid over to the subject of Eddie Murphy and the fact that he was at times called 'a new Richard Pryor.'

'I'm gonna kill him,' Richard Pryor told the millions of viewers.

At that time, they had only met once. It was during 1982 when they happened to be aboard the same airplane.

They talked some, and Eddie says that Richard Pryor made a joking pass at his girlfriend and then fell asleep. However, they did agree to meet and get to know each other.

'Thrilled? I was so thrilled I couldn't stop smiling for weeks,' says Eddie.

People Magazine reported in the summer of 1983 that the meeting between the two black superstars, a meeting that lasted three whole days, had come to pass.

It took place at Richard's home in San Fernando Valley outside Los Angeles.

They went driving in Richard's black VW Rabbit (he has a yellow Rolls Royce also, but they left that one at home).

They shopped together, they got hair cuts, they went out to eat.

They even went to L.A.'s Comedy Store where Richard was trying out some material, after which he handed the mike to Eddie.

A friendship was born during those days. A friendship that both of them acknowledge could not have taken place a few years earlier, not while Richard was heavily into drugs.

'Drugs only allow for relationships with drugs,' is how Richard puts it.

But since 1980, when Richard Pryor was excessively burned (allegedly in connection with freebasing), he has changed. He is mellower. He doesn't joke about drugs as he used to.

The two of them – at the time one was 22, the other 42 – found things that were different and things they have in common. Also, they do see themselves in each other . . .

Eddie Murphy acknowledges constantly that his roots are inside Pryor's material and style. Pryor in turn acknowledges that Bill Cosby paved the way for him, as Dick Gregory paved the way for Bill Cosby.

Their backgrounds are widely different.

Richard Pryor had the rougher road to travel, practically growing up in a brothel, leaving school at 14, going into the army, feeling anger exploding inside him.

He has been married at least four times, has four kids.

57

He has made about thirty movies and twenty albums and has five Grammys . . .

Pryor went through hell to gain public acceptance. Eddie just went *boom!*

Together, they discussed why serious black actors don't get the kind of motion picture deals that the two of them get. Eddie complained on behalf of actors such as Billy Dee Williams and Howard Rollins. The search is not on for new black actors, apparently, while new white actors crop up every year.

Comedy is different, they concluded. 'It's not threatening,' suggested Pryor.

But perhaps the two of them could change things around somewhat . . . by uniting forces in a dramatic film? They have talked about all kinds of possibilities.

Eddie's nickname for Richard Pryor is Yoda (as in the Jedi sage). He does a perfect Yoda imitation: 'You must learn all you can, Eddie. Take all you can learn.'

Eddie Murphy, America's top performer, a black superhero who is not defined by race or class, a man who personifies the meaning of 'being funny' with his endless resilience, the timing that no Swiss could improve on, the tremendous self-confidence that must never distort itself into arrogance, and the quality defying definition, the charm, the gift from the gods . . .

He would get a kick out of becoming *the* big international star . . . and it is happening.

His kicks are his goals, to reach higher, to do more . . . and his kinship is with all human beings striving to create something different and magical and sensational.

LOVING LOVER

To be in love is the best.
—*Eddie Murphy*

There is something undoubting, unblinking, uncompromising, and *unafraid* in Eddie Murphy's attitude towards love as it shines through his words. An attitude that feels right . . . but one that many may expect from a man who has lived more years on earth.

Though he talks a lot about getting girls and constantly points out that singers have it made ('that Mick Jagger . . . and he's ugly! . . . has women running after him . . . '), he seems to desire a close relationship, built on respect, trust, and joy, rather than having casual affairs all over the place.

Many pretend to be cool and show us casual attitudes, but when push comes to shove (when lust comes to love?), who would wish to love any less than totally? Who would have a love that is not true?

Don't most of us want and seek and hope for the real thing?

All signs indicate that Eddie Murphy does.

Love is his thing.

He ended a year-long engagement in October of 1982. The young lady was Shirley Fowler, a student of social work at the University of Pittsburgh. He doesn't discuss it, it's past history, and Eddie is not the kiss-and-tell type.

He is now engaged to a striking-looking young woman, Lisa Figueroa, a straight A-biology (premed) major at Long Island's Adelphi University.

Both of them happily confirm their engagement, but both of them also state that there are no wedding bells in the immediate future.

'There is time,' both say.

They met at a disco.

'Nobody had to introduce them,' says someone who was present that night. 'They just looked at each other . . . as if they *recognised* each other.'

'Definitely love at first sight. And then it grew stronger with every look,' says a close friend of both.

'It wasn't that Eddie was a celebrity either,' another friend points out. 'Lisa is a girl with an identity of her own. She has plans for her future. She has ambitions. She doesn't need to be someone's wife . . . or girlfriend . . . to feel that she is someone . . . '

What does Eddie find special about Lisa outside of obvious good looks?

In a candid interview in *Cosmopolitan*, he attempts to explain.

'She's a good girl. She engages on every level. I can talk to her, hang out, she's funny. And you know how I always say eventually my wife is going to be a submissive woman? She is the exact opposite of that. She's like a female me. Her sense of humour is not as good as mine, but as far as being pigheaded and wanting her way, Lisa is very much like me.

'In the long run, I have to get my way, and with Lisa it just takes me longer to get it. It's a challenge, not at all a boring relationship.'

They will take their time to let things grow and develop between them, since neither one is in a hurry to get married. They realise that they are both very young. She is three years younger than Eddie.

He says, sounding quite serious, 'I just have to know me better. So I'm waiting to get to know me better . . . '

Though some of his friends report that now and then the idea of marriage comes up in his conversation, and he seems to like the idea of it, more and more.

To a *Rolling Stone* reporter, he said, 'She's great for me. I've had a problem since I was young: If a woman lets me dominate her, I get bored with her really fast.'

In the same interview, he also declared, 'We're gonna have spicy black children . . . ' referring to Lisa's Puerto Rican heritage.

Lisa doesn't go around talking to reporters much. She lets him talk.

She is a classy young lady with no need to use Eddie Murphy to achieve some kind of notoriety.

Other than that, she is highly articulate on many subjects. She is interested in most things and often impresses people with her detailed knowledge of a variety of topics. She has a few close friends, and what they say about her is that she values friendships highly, that she never breaks a promise, and that she is always there if someone needs her.

'Medicine seems natural to her. Her whole personality is one of warmth and understanding. But she's also fun to be around. She is a terrific dancer, she likes movies . . . Well-rounded, I guess describes her,' says a friend of Eddie's.

She lives in the Bronx with her family – she lived in the college dorm for a while but missed the family. She studies hard. And whenever she is with Eddie, her fine-featured, exquisite face glows.

So . . . a beautiful girl with brains, a girl who is as

close to her own family as he is to his, a girl with an identity and a will of her own, a girl who values loyalty and honesty . . . that's Eddie Murphy's love. In spite of what he has declared in the past about women . . . But perhaps he was just kidding?

MACHO MALE

Everything!
—*Mae West (when asked what she*
wanted to be remembered for)

No question about it. Spend a few minutes in his company, and you know beyond doubt that Eddie likes the ladies, and the ladies like Eddie.

Playgirl put him on the list of the ten sexiest men in America, and they are really looking hard at men. His response? He laughs. That sucked-in laugh that could pull feathers off a chicken if it came too close.

Is he aware of his sex appeal?

In an interview in *Cosmopolitan*, he appeared rather bashful.

'Ah, other people say that stuff. Girls like me, and if that's sex appeal, I got it. But I don't know how to turn it on and turn it off. I don't walk around like . . . "Hey, I got sex appeal!" . . . with inflated chest and swagger . . . '

How about doing a love story? He is not averse to playing a romantic lead if the movie is right, what he calls a 'character piece with a love interest.'

Some people have asked why there was not a real love story in *Beverly Hills Cop* . . .

'There was talk of putting in a love interest,' he reveals, 'but something like that slows it down. If you're playing cops and robbers, and the cop is chasing the robber but decides to pick up some chick first, it slows the movie down.'

Jamie Lee Curtis has this to say about Eddie since they worked together in *Trading Places:* 'First of all, he's terrific. Just a terrific guy. I was glad to see that in spite of it all, all the fuss and the fame, he was still acting his age. I mean he really digs cars and girls, girls and cars.'

Not for him the current trend of younger men/older women – neither in life nor in the movies. He admires actresses such as Jane Fonda and Meryl Streep, but he points out that his own mother is forty-three.

'I couldn't handle a romantic comedy with someone who's, what's Jane Fonda, forty-nine?'

'I like women in general,' he'll say. 'But basically, I like women who are younger than me.'

But once he did have a relationship with an older woman.

'Yeah. But just one. She was thirty-six. I was twenty-one. But you know, women are women. It was no different. We had the same arguments.'

His friends kidded him and kept asking him what he had learned, but he says that she didn't have a thing to teach him. 'Women are women.'

He says that what attracts him in women are 'pretty faces, pretty figures, and pretty feet.'

He has this thing about small feet.

'Big feet . . . turn me off. And I don't like corns. No bunions. You know how the toenail polish be chipping off? I *hate* that.'

Smokers need not apply either.

'I've seen women gorgeous beyond compare, but if they smoke, I will not approach them. I *hate* cigarette breath.'

Above: Sophisticated Eddie at the 1983 Grammy Awards
(CHARLES ADAMS)

Overleaf: As Lt. Landry, driver of the 'annihilator' supertank
in *Best Defense*
(PARAMOUNT PICTURES)

Above: Eddie with Nick Nolte in Eddie's first film, *48 hours*
(PARAMOUNT PICTURES)

eaf: Eddie with Ola Ray in *48 hours*
(CE McBROOM)

Above: Eddie and Nick Nolte in *48 hours*
(BRUCE McBROOM)

If one tries to discuss issues related to the women's liberation movement, he is ready.

Having made the customary declaration that in the work place, it's the competency that counts and that, naturally, equal pay for equal work is only fair, he'll go on to the personal side of things.

'I'm pretty old-fashioned. I'm your basic average everyday guy, and I know women don't like to read it, but I feel like a woman can have some say in what goes on in the relationship, but the guy is the core of it, and what I say goes. That's the kind of woman I'll wind up with, someone who's willing to let me call most of the shots.'

Hear that, Lisa?

He laughs. 'Well, Lisa . . . now . . . that's a little different . . . '

If the talk goes on to popular music stars, the andryogynous kind, he'll say, 'Fine . . . Fine with me. But let's talk about Elvis Presley and the reason he was king . . . '

He'll discuss why Elvis was the biggest musical star ever.

'Because he looked like a guy, sang like a guy, and came off like a guy. Guys liked him, women liked him, little kids wanted to be like him. He had enormous crossover appeal.'

He says that he wants kids 'real bad,' but he has definite ideas about bringing them up.

'I want my boys to wear men's clothes and my daughters to wear women's. And if I had a son and he was watching some guy making music on television, and he came downstairs with makeup on and his mother's shoes and said, I want to be like so-and-so, I'd beat the shit out of him!'

He feels it must be very confusing for little kids to grow up and not quite know what is what so far as the sexes are concerned.

Do macho men fight?

There was a much-publicised brawl in a West Hollywood nightclub (Carlos & Charlie) on the night of July 14, 1984.

Some conflicting statements have been made – some even hinted that Eddie perhaps was not totally sober. Let's see if we can get the facts straight, as straight as they can be if one was not right there, taking notes.

First of all, he was sober. As is customary for him (and not always great for restaurant and nightclub owners), he only had a soft drink or mineral water. He doesn't drink.

Eddie Murphy was upstairs in the private disco club with his entourage.

Downstairs a group of six people were having dinner.

After dinner, the six were invited upstairs. They went upstairs.

As they entered, Eddie made a comment about the wife of one of the men. What kind of comment? Flirtatious? Insulting? Just a joke? Whatever he said, the husband didn't like it. By the way, it is believed by an impartial observer that the man did not know that this was Eddie Murphy. To him it was just a guy who made some remark about his wife, and he did not like it.

He pushed Eddie.

Eddie is not a fighter. He doesn't like fights. The whole thing could have ended right there.

But the people in Eddie's entourage did not like seeing Eddie pushed. Instead of quieting everybody down and even getting Eddie out of there, the people with him began hitting and pushing the man. A regular brawl ensued.

Eddie was not participating. Then somebody happened to hit him, and he received a split lip. He picked up a glass and threw it. 'He didn't throw it at the man it hit,' says one woman. 'He just flared up and threw it. It hit a man and cut his wrist or arm slightly.'

But throwing glasses is not lawful. A glass is a weapon, says the law.

Police came. Eddie left (no, he was not arrested). There may or may not be a lawsuit or two as a result. But to a great extent, it seems a case of making a goose out of a feather.

Another version (there are several) of the evening goes briefly like this. A young woman, Azra, was insulted by a man. This (unidentified) man pursued her. She hid behind Eddie. In the ensuing scuffle, both Murphy and Phillip Shumway, a bystander who tried to break up the fight, suffered minor injuries.

A fight breaks out, there is confusion, eyewitnesses give different reports, according to what they believe to have happened.

'Eddie is not the type to get involved in bar fights. I mean, for heaven's sake, the guy doesn't even drink. Not ever.'

So speaks a friend of his, and her sentiments are echoed by hosts of other people who know Eddie.

'He doesn't like to see a woman insulted, though,' says one woman friend. 'For that matter, he doesn't like to see anyone insulted. What he did, he did protectively. He wouldn't stand there and make derogatory remarks about a woman who walked into a place.'

Eddie has been back to the same place after the incident, always drinking just his regular soft drink.

'You sure don't make a lot of money on him,' kids one of the owners of the place, who also finds him utterly pleasant, warm, polite, and more quiet than she would have expected.

How macho is he? Whatever the term means . . .

His humour can get rough at times, as we all know, but there remains that twinkle and that . . . yes, innocence . . . that makes you want to root for him.

Whatever he says about women, most women do not feel that he's on the other side of some fence, wanting to maintain some kind of traditional masculine superiority.

'You can't nowadays, anyhow,' he says. 'All the women are into aerobics and stuff. They fight back!'

One girl who dated him before he met Lisa says, 'Going out with Eddie was great. Because of the way he is. Not because he can afford to take you to elegant places . . . We didn't go to elegant places. We went to a movie, we went for ice cream . . . or a hamburger. But he *talks* to you. So many big shots talk *at* you. Not Eddie. He wants to know what you think and how you feel, and he listens to what you have to say. Funny? Yes, he's funny but not compulsively funny. And he doesn't sit there and talk about himself all the time, either. Eddie is . . . Eddie is a guy who likes women. And you know, a lot of men dig women sexually, but they don't really *like* us . . . '

All right, Eddie Murphy today likes women (Walter Hill said about him in the pre-Lisa days: 'Eddie can hear the rustle of nylon stockings at 50 yards') – and women find him immensely attractive.'

Don't know how he will feel about this, but let us reveal what we have been told: This is a more recent development than he likes to admit!

He was no teenage Romeo, after all!

Old schoolmates of his insist that he was a bit too much of a show-off for the girls to really go for him.

One girl tells how he could mimic everyone. 'He was fantastic, but I know several girls who rejected him because they thought he was too silly!'

The boys liked him better than the girls – they liked his constant jokes and clowning. Some of the girls insist that it was because of the boys he was voted the school's most popular student in 1979.

'Girls don't like non-stop jokes,' says one.

But another girl who knew him back then says, 'I always thought he was special, somehow. In my case, I would have loved to have gone out with him. But he

68

intimidated me. I mean, here is a guy who cracks a joke a minute – what do you talk to him about? When he didn't go on a joke binge, he was one of the quietest people I know. He seemed . . . preoccupied . . . '

With his kind of ambition, he must not have had time to develop the lifestyle and manners of the 'macho' male.

NECESSITIES AND NEEDS

Money doesn't make anyone happy,
but I'd rather cry in a Jaguar
than in a bus.
—*Francoise Sagan*

'I don't need much,' said Eddie Murphy to a friend.
'How much does one man need . . . ?'

It is true that his life lacks the ostentatious lustre of
many stars.

He has not chosen to live in a secluded, palm-embraced
mansion in Bel Air nor in a fancy penthouse in Manhattan. His home is suburban New Jersey, and his house
was to a great extent decorated by his mother.

On the other hand, it isn't exactly modest either, unless
you call a rambling, five-bedroom affair modest. It is
located in Alpine (that's in New Jersey, just north of the
George Washington Bridge into Manhattan), and it is
done in contemporary decor. White walls, glass and polished metal surfaces – everything is smooth and polished.

Towering, ivied oaks shade the house, the lawn is
perfectly manicured. Electronic gates protect from
unwelcome visitors. (And there are quite a few of those –
young girls with important messages, for instance.)

The tennis court has a basketball hoop at each end . . . Of course, he has a swimming pool. Also a gym in the basement for working out.

In one corner of the white-on-white living room with couches that envelop you as you sit down, there is a life-size image of him done in black leather. In one corner, a gigantic movie poster dominates . . . All over the walls, there are magazine cover pictures, all featuring a certain (and usually happily grinning) Edward Regan Murphy . . . Lately, we hear that Lisa's picture has gone up on the wall. ('I have to put some pictures of my family up there, too.')

He has a Kawai baby grand piano . . . There is a recreation room with wall-screen television and a bank of stereo equipment. He has drums, amplifiers, electric guitars, and keyboards in a rather small room where he spends much time composing and playing, often with neighbour Joe Piscopo bashing the drums.

He has a pet parrot who hollers 'Hey, sucker!' to anyone who seems to fit.

The master bedroom features a king-size brass bed, pleated satin canopy on the ceiling, and a stuffed giant gorilla that a friend gave him.

When Barbara Walters interviewed Eddie Murphy on her special, she asked what he does when he is beset by problems like everyone else.

'I go out and polish my car,' said he.

But which car?

It seems, by latest reports, that he owns six cars. That would be one Rolls-Royce, a red Porsche 928 (cost: $43,000) equipped with seventeen speakers (!), a Corvette, a white limousine, a Ferrari, a custom-made Spartan, a black $36,000 Jaguar XJS. Which seems to make seven! Perhaps he has sold one, given one away . . . But he owns just about half a dozen cars, none of which qualifies in the economy car category.

He has also given his mother a Datsun 200 SX while

Vernon received a Lincoln with a six-speaker sound system.

Eddie Murphy likes cars.

But why did he not choose to live in some exclusive part of Los Angeles, rubbing elbows with other stars under the grapefruit sun constantly shining through the smog and bouncing off the windshields of the more than four million automobiles in the county?

'It has to do with sanity,' suggests a friend, reminding us of Jack Lemmon's quip: 'Hollywood is a wonderful place. Just don't let yourself know that you've decided to stay here!'

'Staying close to your roots may help you not to lose yourself,' says another.

Eddie Murphy gives the impression that he has kept his sanity in spite of the whirlwind success.

At first, the sudden money gave Eddie a jolt. His initial success on *Saturday Night Live*, which meant large weekly pay cheques, threw him for a (short-lasting) loop.

'All money and no responsibilities . . . '

He was still living at home then.

'I spent like a madman. I'd pick up the cheque at a restaurant for ten people. My mother would ask me to take out the garbage, so I'd throw her a hundred dollars, and she'd say, "Okay, your little brother can take out the garbage." '

But he saw what he was doing. And he understood it.

'It's okay to lose your mind for a little while, because you're only going to be twenty-one once. I don't drink, but I run around a lot. My only vices are cars and jewellery – rings and necklaces, nothing too gaudy.'

When he moved away from home and into his own apartment, he selected one that was located only minutes from home.

'I'm childish when it comes to Mommy. She's still gotta be nearby.'

He admits easily that he *needs* his family and his old

friends. Most of his friends are not Hollywood people but old buddies from his Long Island high school. One exception is the rubber-faced comic actor Joe Piscopo (also from *Saturday Night Live*), ten years older than Eddie, and definitely one of his closest friends.

As has anyone who has taken the jet-blast ride to stardom, Eddie Murphy gets the usual star treatment from many directions. People tend to pamper him, agree with him, cater to his whims, spoil him, tell him that he's fantastic, wonderful, terrific, that he can do no wrong. That is why he needs the casual tone from his family and old friends. The 'hey' Eddie, cut it out!' type of things if and when arrogance sets in.

Clinton Smith is one of his oldest friends. (That's whose house he used to sneak over to in order to get some sleep when his parents wanted him to keep 'decent hours' and get out of the house in the mornings.) Another close and equally old friend is Derrick Lawrence, who is also his bodyguard, a man who has a black belt in karate. (In Eddie's situation, you do need a bodyguard.)

Derrick loves Eddie Murphy. 'I'd been laid off my job,' says he, who is married and has children. 'Eddie came and asked me if I wanted to work for him. I love Eddie for it and I always will. I'm like his Knight of the Round Table. I'll serve him till the day I die.'

Bodyguard he needs but maids he does without.

There are no maids, no butler, in his house.

He fends for himself. Though sometimes the only thing you'd find if you opened the refrigerator in his home is the light bulb.

This millionaire may have dinner in his spotless kitchen, feasting on an extra large hamburger with cheese, French fries, and a strawberry milkshake.

Oh yes, it is absolutely true that he does not drink at all, not even beer. He even prefers herbal tea to coffee (though he does take sugar in his tea).

He likes to be alone quite a bit. He watches movies on television, studying, thinking. He watches very few sports events. 'I can't stand seeing other people excel at something I can't do,' says he, who is in great shape but never was into sports per se.

Like most of us, he likes to have a good time, but that does not necessarily mean swanky parties and constant attention. He is in show business to work, not to swagger around, playing at being a star, feeding an ego. Insecure people have ego problems, and insecure he is not.

He thoroughly enjoys the luxuries his success has brought him. But he also sees clearly what his real necessities are.

'My needs have to do with love and growth . . . not with things . . . '

OUT-TAKES
AND OPPONENTS

He was no genius so of course
he had no enemies.
—*Oscar Wilde*

Most popular, oh yes! But naturally that does not mean that everybody, without exception, loves Eddie Murphy.

Not only the gay community has been offended by some of his material; quite a few others find it, at least in part, coarse and too profanity-loaded.

Seventy-one-year-old veteran comedian Red Skelton calls Eddie Murphy wonderful but adds 'he doesn't need to use four-letter words.'

That sentiment is echoed by other (older) comedians.

'Quite a few find his favourite twelve-letter word a bit worn, you know, the one which begins with 'mother' and ends with 'er'.

'I like to say it right off,' Murphy sometimes tells his audiences. 'To show that we are all family here.'

'Eddie is one of the funniest men alive, but his language grows tedious,' says one colleague of his.

75

'He needs more of a theme now,' says another. 'An expletive now and then can add spice, but he overuses. He has funny material, really funny material. I like his comparisons of white, black and Chinese behinds, for instance, but I find his jokes about flatulence in the bath-tub a bit on the childish side. Though a lot of his audience is very young, and they love it.'

And though he has made three hit movies with rave reviews, *Best Defence* (summer of 1984) is certainly a certifiable stinker, as Eddie himself is the first to point out.

There are even some who are less than enthusiastic about him as an actor, though they usually add that he definitely has a lot of talent. The main complaint from these is that he has largely played the same character so far; always cheeky, always glib, always moving fast on his feet. 'In a sense, he has remained a stand-up comic in his movies,' someone said. 'Now, let's see if the guy can act.'

That's one opinion and not a widespread one, quoted mainly to point out that everybody does not agree, not even when it comes to Eddie Murphy.

Eddie has come under attack from members of the black community for some of his work such as 'that pimp thing, Velvet Jones. The identification with negative stereotypes is still there, and it shouldn't be,' says one. And goes on, 'It's just unthinking man, in this day and age, to even fool around with stereotypes like the pimp or the drug pusher. The question is, does the guy have any social consciousness?'

The revival of the character Buckwheat with his dumb grin and inability to pronounce consonants correctly has also drawn criticism. As has his frequent use of black dialect.

One opinion: 'Because black audiences are so acutely sensitised to the few images presented about themselves on television, we tend to want our performers to be real,

76

to be "black": yet we don't want them to look laughable in front of white folks making *us* laugh.'

Eddie listens to criticism. He knows that he is growing up and changing, that he is developing certain sensitivities, some of which simply take time and living to develop.

But his comments also make sense. 'I do Buckwheat because I think it's funny, and the character is too absurd, abstract, and ridiculous to be taken seriously. White people don't look at Buckwheat and say, "Yes, that's the way blacks dress and act." It's stuff like *The Jeffersons* that's a step back for blacks.'

Another time he said, 'What's so bad about doing black dialect if black dialect exists?'

Or, 'I cannot see how blacks can watch a show like *Diff'rent Strokes* or *The Jeffersons* and then say my characters are demeaning . . . My characters are real!'

White people have opinions on the matter, too.

New York film critic Pauline Kael wrote:

'White people couldn't really learn anything of what it is to be black from Eddie Murphy; he is playing off their ideas of what it is to be black.'

Though another writer, Julia Cameron, commented in an article entitled *Murphy's Law as seen in the movies:*

'With Eddie Murphy, it is possible for a white audience to make believe that we're all in this together – that it is not as simple as black and white.' She ends the article: 'But look twice. His comedy is serious business. Eddie Murphy has a (funny) bone to pick with us.'

Get out in the spotlight and take your chances, that's how it is.

Eddie Murphy knows this. He knows that there is no way to please everybody, that whatever he does, there will be various reactions. He is not afraid of creating a bit of controversy . . . or even of making mistakes and offending. He feels it is a matter of growth which basically means constant changing.

The private Eddie Murphy is a man who values friendships highly and who has a natural respect for others, and comments from people who know him well or just a little tend to be highly favourable.

Just to get some variation on the theme, we tried to get some other kinds of comments, to find the warts, so to speak. Of course, he does not behave like an angel at all times, in all places. He has his moods. There have been complaints when he has not shown up for an appearance or been late. A few months ago, for instance, he had promised to appear at the Comic Strip Club. People waited. No Eddie Murphy. It turned out that he and Lisa had gone off to a movie instead.

A funny, lovable guy . . . a human being with some quirks like the rest of us . . .

A human being intent on growing . . .

PRANKS AND PEOPLE

As merry as the day is long.
—*Shakespeare*

From stand-up comic to television star to movie star –
Eddie Murphy's leap from one medium to another seems
natural.

A look around reveals that this does not happen that
often: a comic may not always a movie star make.

It has worked for those who developed definite, well-
defined personalities on television, such as Goldie
Hawn, the wacky blonde with the high-pitched laughter,
Chevy Chase with his air of overgrown college boy, and
Bill Murray, the spaced-out party boy. But others did not
make it, in spite of tremendous talents. Sid Caesar, Carol
Burnett, Lily Tomlin and quite a few others with high
energy and the abilty to create memorable characters, a
multitude of funny figures, had surprising trouble really
making it on the big screen in one role, one character.
Eddie is one of the few of those able to do a gallery of
characters who also easily slid into the movie star image.

In *48 Hrs.* he played a convict sprung from prison for

79

just forty-eight hours to help tough cop Nick Nolte catch a couple of killers.

The director, Walter Hill, is an unafraid man. He had seen Eddie on *Saturday Night Live* and, though knowing that Eddie had never made a movie, felt that his talent was of the kind closer to an actor than to a joke teller and quick-change artist. The experiment worked, indeed. (The scene in which Eddie takes charge in a redneck bar is already considered something of a classic.)

Though Eddie says that he was probably about the fifth choice for the part. 'I think I came after Gregory Hines and Howard Rollins and at least a couple of others.'

Director Walter Hill comments, 'Eddie's not just a gifted comedian doing a star turn. He's got such a strong centre, a strong feeling for who he is . . . he's remarkable.'

The actress Gloria Gifford had the pleasure of working with Eddie Murphy when he was just two weeks old as a movie actor. She came in to read for a part (as his girlfriend) in *48 Hrs.* She had never met Eddie before, but as she walked in and greeted him, he began to give her back her own role in *California Suite* in which she played Richard Pryor's wife. She was flabbergasted. There were her lines, her inflections. It turned out that he had seen the movie several times.

'It was incredible,' she comments.

The part was not right for Gloria, and she figured that that was it. Then she received a call from her agent. Would she play a small part, that of a hooker, in the film? She said yes, when she heard that Eddie Murphy had written the scene after he had met her.

'He saw an actress he respected who wasn't right for that particular part so he created another part. It's indeed unique and wonderful,' says she.

The whole thing became a highly pleasant experience due to Eddie's warmth and that of his friends around

Trading Places: Eddie sitting in as a musician and *below* with Dan Aykroyd
(PARAMOUNT PICTURES)

Trading Places: Eddie with Jamie Lee Curtis, Dan Aykroyd and Denholm Elliott and below as a blind Vietnam veteran (PARAMOUNT PICTURES)

Beverly Hills Cop: Eddie with Lisa Eilbacher and *overleaf* with Lisa Eilbacher and Judge Reinhold
(PARAMOUNT PICTURES)

Eddie with Rebbie Jackson
(CRAIG ANTHONY/COLUMBIA PICTURES)

Eddie with fellow comedian/actor Richard Pryor
(MARK SENNET/SHOOTING STAR)

him. 'They created an air of festivity. It was as if they reminded us all that we are supposed to have fun while working.'

She is impressed by Eddie's big heart. 'He's a real gentleman. You can't help but love him. He's so easy to meet, so open. I felt immediate rapport with him. I'd work with him any time, in a large or a small part. Because it's just so much fun to work with Eddie, to be around him.'

As Billy Ray Valentine in *Trading Places*, Eddie impersonated an exchange student from Cameroon in Africa and a bantam rooster practising kung fu. He also transformed himself from social parasite to soigné aristocrat.

Ralph Bellamy, the veteran actor who co-stars in the movie, has this to say: 'He did these roles as if he'd been in the business all his life. He's like an old-timer. He has professional confidence without intruding on the scene or script . . . He looked at Don Ameche and me, not to learn from us, but so as not to take anything away, not to steal a scene. It's rare.'

No black actor has come on the scene as fast as Eddie, not since Bill Cosby more than twenty years ago.

Joe Piscopo, who was Murphy's partner for three and a half years on *Saturday Night Live* and who is a close friend as well as a neighbour, has followed Eddie's career in detail.

At one time, he said, 'It's true in a way that Eddie is actually playing himself on-screen. He manages to be totally natural and relaxed. I'd also like to see him try something more serious . . . something with Scorcese or Coppola. *I* know he can pull it off, but I'm not sure *he* does.'

Watching him any time, any place, one notices the perception that is always at work whenever he comes in contact with people . . . It's almost uncanny the way he has of noticing things, unsaid things, non-obvious things . . . all fuel for that artistic fire.

Sometimes he uses this ability privately in joking with his friends, hitting the nail on the head, going right for the kill. But he is not one to use his perception about people to hurt those around him, to point out weak points about which they may be sensitive.

Neither is he a wild prankster, forever playing tricks on his friends.

Actually, he is rather quiet in private. A silent observer a good deal of the time . . .

He remains fascinated by people, by what makes them tick, what makes them angry or elated. He is interested in how anger and hang-ups and stereotypal thinking can be translated into laughter, a laughter that may be the needed release.

He may affect our view of things.

QUICK QUIPS

An artist will betray himself
by some sort of sincerity.
—*G.K. Chesterton*

'It's more than a game now. It's business.'

'I'm a happy guy.'

'If I want to be a dramatic actor, I just put on the sunglasses and turn into Billy Dee Williams.'

'I know I want to make something of myself.'

'One virtue that I have . . . I'm not indecisive . . . '

'My comedy's good-time comedy.'

'There's a million guys out there like me. I was just fortunate. I was in the right place at the right time and said the right thing. And had a charming smile.'

'The Pope . . . he's tough. The Pope went to Harlem. Now I'm a black man and *I* don't even go to Harlem . . . '

'I went to Texas, though, looking for racism . . . Ready for it . . . But they didn't have none at the time . . . '

'I'm real secure with myself, within myself . . . '

'I hold on to my reality. My reality is where I came

83

from. My family. I can get real pompous and arrogant if I'm away from my reality too long.'

'Yeah, I've had some success . . . You know, if it all went away tomorrow, I could take it. I've done what I wanted to do . . . and I've made a little money . . . '

'Man, I've only just begun . . . I want to do everything!'

'I have a filthy mouth, did you notice?'

'I'm just trying to get a laugh.'

'Life . . . is too precious . . . too precious to kill yourself slowly by doing drugs . . . '

'Whatever everybody else's doing has never been hip to me.'

'Things don't just happen . . . Whatever happens to you, *you* make it happen.'

'I'm not up there to preach with my comedy. I'm up there to get laughs.'

'Laughter and excitement, those are the emotions I want to tap.'

'Like the Beatles were to music, that's what I like to be to comedy.'

'I want to be more than big, I want to be tremendous.'

'I'd hate to be maintstream by age forty, doing President jokes and golf jokes.'

'I have the luxury of being able to experiment.'

'There is very little anger in my humour.'

'Richard is the King. I'll be content with being the Prince.'

'I really think God writes my material.'

'I am not astounded by my talents. I think that I came along at a time when the industry and when black people are reaching out for heroes. It's like I have a warped sense of humour. Every couple of years this country's sense of humour changes. Hipper people are into comedy, not into silly things.'

'It really hasn't changed a lot of things. Hollywood looks at me in a different light. I just happen to be one of those brothers that's getting a break today. My life-style hasn't changed much. I'm not freaking out.'

'Richard is my idol but I want to be the first Eddie Murphy, not another Richard Pryor.'

'All these kids playing video games – boy, I'll tell you, in twenty years we're gonna have a race of destructive kids who are stupid because they didn't go to school. *But* they'll have great reflexes.'

'How I get my material? I live, I watch, I hang out with my friends . . . Material is all around . . . but you never know if it works or not until you stand up on that stage and try it out on an audience.'

'Onstage, my subconscious takes over, and what I'm about comes out.'

'I'm not very political. I don't even vote. The way I see it, the President does what he wants to do, and if we do what we want, we don't have to be affected.'

'I come from a strong black family with a strong mother and a strong father. There was a lot of love in my family.'

RANKING AND RIBBING

My tongue is the pen of
a ready writer.
—*The Bible (Psalms)*

'Ranking,' the art of insults, is a tradition that Eddie grew up with and perfected . . . and keeps working on.

Both of his parents, he says, are champion rankers.

As a boy back then, it was whatever he could think of to say about another boy's brain power, manhood, looks or family, but the idea was to find the right phrase, the cutting tone without being just gross.

An example from his early repertoire: 'Your mama got a wooden leg with a kickstand.'

Today, Eddie Murphy takes his audience for a ride, a vicarious ride on his quick-silver mind, laughing all the way, at everything.

But listen carefully. Eddie's jive is blessedly free from dark malice. Under the insults and the ghetto gutter talk, there lurks a sassy little boy, outfoxing the grownups at a game he has been practising all his life.

He is Little Rascal playing Dirty Harry . . . and winning!

End result is that people just love him. Or as Robert Wachs gauges his appeal, 'People want to gift-wrap him and take him home.'

And yet, nobody and nothing is safe around Eddie.

He finds the exaggerated swagger of a dressed-to-the-teeth black man on a city street as funny as the pompous, rigid 'Marlboro men' in Washington.

How can people take themselves so bloody seriously? he seems to be asking.

His most successful take-off routines have dealt with this.

Sometimes his satire may border on the dangerous. Examples such as the militant film critic Raheem Abdul Muhammad and the white-hating Tyrone Green come to mind.

George Orwell said that 'a man wears a mask, and his face grows to fit it.' In the finest moments in Eddie's sharp-eyed comedy routines, he illustrates the ridiculous-ness of masks and poses, of our fears to be what we are. And thereby, he gives us glimpses of a world where we wouldn't need any masks. A world without hypocrisy.

'I don't want to sound like some Zen Buddhist fool,' he said in an interview, 'but I think you do a lot to create your own reality.'

He dares to do the unexpected.

He has walked onto stages, looked out over a mixed audience and said, looking serious, 'Okay, okay, let's get all this out of our systems right now. On the count of three, I want you all to scream "nigger" . . . '

He has gone on to play with a partly shocked audience, warning them that other words would not be allowed. 'No coon, no Alabama porch monkey . . . Just give me straight "nigger" on the count of three.'

And then he has begun counting.

After one, there is usually a strange, loaded silence.

After two . . . nervous giggles as people sneak looks at each other, eager to find out how their neighbours react.

'Two and a half'' with a drum roll . . .

People readying themselves, still not knowing what is the 'right' thing to do.

'Three: NIGGER!'

People actually screaming along with him . . .

Then . . . a dead silence.

Then laughter. Waves of laughter rolling over the room.

Relief.

Applause.

He has them in his hand now, easy to shape as clay, his to do anything he wants with. Now, they'll follow wherever he goes.

Sometimes he has taken an audience all the way to the end, and then, as suddenly, changed his mind.

'Wait a minute, I ain't gonna let you scream that shit!'

This is one routine he wanted to do on the *Tonight Show*. How about *that?!* Asking TV audiences to scream the forbidden word 'nigger' . . . '

The idea was, not surprisingly, rejected.

It is not the only idea of his that has not been deemed acceptable for television.

Other rejects are 'The Golden Age School of Obedience' with grandparents being disciplined ('See, you can't beat up kids on TV – but you can beat up old people . . . ') . . . 'Mr. T. Meets E.T.' and the big guy really goes after the little alien . . . Or 'Kung Fu Classroom' where teachers would kick little girls through the walls . . .

'My comedy is wild and dangerous,' says Eddie. 'I like people to think of me as a comic who takes chances. Richard Pryor is where he is now because of dangerous comedy.'

Saturday Night Live offered him many chances to do outrageous things, but he reached a point where he felt the need for a change, for a move in another direction. The show became too restrictive for his brand of humour. While he never will forget what the show did for him, he did feel good about leaving, from an artistic point of view. On February 25, 1984, he did his last show. He did make a return appearance after he had quit, and it was one of the show's absolutely highest rated programmes.

He brought everything with him to the movies, not the least his concern to deliver a polished, top performance whatever he does.

He took off, facing the future fearlessly.

The reviewer Pauline Kael said after his first film, '[Murphy is] fastidious, and with timing so precise that it seems almost surgical . . . '

That perfect timing and the special delivery with rapid, distinct gestures means that some of his stuff is considerably less funny when reproduced on a printed page.

But there is one take-off that somehow illustrates how his mind works. He pretends that he is driving along with Stevie Wonder and talking to him.

'All right, Stevie . . . so you're such a genius . . . great . . . your music and all . . . So what? Think it impresses me? . . . That doesn't impress me . . . Want to impress me? Huh? Okay, take the wheel for a while!'

If all he had to work with was a shock effect due to his spicy language, it would have worn thin by now. Shock effect wears off. But luckily, for us and for him, Eddie Murphy is a lot more than a certain few words, which is why we keep watching him.

In many of his sketches, we hear the street talk and those words and all that . . . but we also pick up the inner-city demand for respect and the human qualities that we can identify with.

So much is said about young people adoring Eddie, that we wish to quote a lady of age sixty-nine. She says, 'You don't even feel he's coarse. You just giggle. He's not *bad*, just naughty . . . Sure, he uses dirty words . . . but better dirty words and clean living than the other way around. I don't think he's such a bad influence. Listen, every kid knows these words . . . And I think he may move away from the gutter language when he grows tired of it . . . or when he senses that people get tired of it . . . '

Somehow, Eddie is extremely *now* . . . with his own vocabulary, his own way of saying and doing things . . . everything punctuated by that barking-seal-in-the-sun-on-a-smooth-cliff laughter of his . . . *huryk* . . . *huryk* . . . *huryk* . . .

SWEET SOFTNESS

Nothing is so strong as gentleness;
nothing so gentle as real strength.
—*Francis de Sales*

There are other sides and aspects of Eddie Murphy's persona than the fast-talking street-smart guy.

His album on CBS Records, due out soon, will reveal some such sides.

'How could it be' . . . a ballad of lost love . . . 'You are my life' . . . a reggae-flavoured love song . . . 'I me us we' . . . a gospel-inspired number about tolerance and brotherhood . . .

By the way, his singing voice is a bit higher than one would expect . . . shades of Stevie Wonder . . . His style is smooth, smooth, smooth . . .

There is also a song entitled 'C-o-n confused . . . '

'I write a lot of songs about people being confused,' he says. 'People are.'

He has also admitted to being nervous about the album and its reception. 'I'm treading unknown ground here . . . ' Then he laughs. 'But if it doesn't work, I can always use it in my future comic acts . . . Say, remember a couple of years back when I tried to make an album? Terrible . . . '

Eddie Murphy has enormous personal charm – his mother calls it a special 'sweetness' – that makes people want to be with him, warm themselves close to him.

Perhaps the clue is his eyes. They never lose their warmth, they never stop smiling. Whatever he says, however outrageous, the eyes reveal that he is just kidding, that he is laughing on the inside.

When the Hollywood makeup artists decided to choose the twelve most hypnotic eyes – twelve eyes equal six pairs – Eddie Murphy was one of the six because of the 'dancing mischief' in those big brown peepers.

His friend Joe Piscopo has said, 'I'd like to get away with what he gets away with but I can't. Know why he does? Because he has enormous vulnerability. When he smiles, you want this kid to be your son . . . ' Or brother . . . or friend . . . or lover . . .

His co-star in *48 Hrs.*, Nick Nolte, pointed out that with some people you feel an immediate like, with others an as immediate dislike. 'The chemistry between us worked. He is one of the most likeable guys.'

Dan Aykroyd (*Trading Places*) is no less enthusiastic. 'We trade concepts and ideas, and I would work with him again, anytime, anyplace.'

Veteran actors Ralph Bellamy and Don Ameche (also *Trading Places*) have plenty of fond words for him. Eddie totally broke them up at one time. That was when he discovered that Bellamy had made ninety-nine films and Ameche forty-nine. Amazed, he slapped his thigh. 'That means between the three of us, we've made one hundred and fifty films!'

Even hardheaded critics admit that they see and fall for the special Murphy sweetness.

'Murphy exudes the kind of cheeky, cocky charm that has been missing from the screen since Cagney was a pup, snarling his way out of the ghetto,' wrote Richard

Schickel in *Time*. 'But as befits a manchild of the soft-spoken '80s, there is an insinuating sweetness about the heart that is always visible on the sleeve of Murphy's habitual sweatshirt. It is discernible not only by adolescent females but by case-hardened critics as well.'

'My favourite story about Eddie,' says Bob Wachs, 'is that when you scratch the surface, he's the same as he's always been. There's a levelness to him, a niceness, a warmth toward his family and friends that has absolutely not changed. He still maintains the same friendships he had in high school. You don't see Eddie Murphy hanging out with celebrities and excluding his friends. Eddie Murphy has always taken his whole crowd of friends around with him.'

Finally, a word from his mother – and who knows him better?

'Nobody wants to believe me when I tell them that Eddie has not changed. But he hasn't. Fame didn't change him. He was a good boy then, and he's a good boy now.'

He is great with little kids . . . tender with animals . . .

Eddie Murphy is a gentle man.

TALKATIVE
AND TRUTHFUL

My way of joking is to tell
the truth. It's the funniest
joke in the world.
—*G.B. Shaw*

Eddie Murphy tells it like he sees it.

There is a directness, a basic honesty, in him that is appealing.

And, of course, there is that easy self-confidence about him that shines through in all his work as well as in interviews and appearances, a confidence that has to do with somehow knowing himself, having a centre, not being afraid to give of himself in many directions.

But call him a genius and see him stop dead in his tracks.

'I tell a good joke,' he says. 'But there's no such thing as a comic genius. Geniuses are people who do things with their brains – scientists, people with academic training. Not guys who play piano or make people laugh. I'd be the first to admit that I'm a very funny guy, and the last to admit that I'm a genius.'

He questions sometimes our need to have idols, people

who are more than people we admire, people who are godlike and superhuman. He laughs and declares that this does not describe him.

'All I want to say is that I'm just as screwed up as everybody else,' he told *Newsweek*. 'No better. No worse. I'm just as capable of sinning or of doing good as anybody else. I've done some real mean shit, and I've done some kind things, too.'

He baulks a bit at the opinion that as a black entertainer, he carries an extra load of responsibility and has to watch his every syllable, every act.

'I won't do anything that's degrading to me or my people, but I don't feel like I'm here to break new ground . . . I'm not the Saviour. I'm just a brother that God happened to give a little talent to, and I just happened to luck out and get into showbusiness, and I tell jokes, and if they get laughs, *fine,* and if they don't get laughs, *fine.* I'll work on it.'

That sounds humble enough. How does it go with his image of being a bit cocky? He shrugs and admits that he is that, too.

'There's no such thing in this business as someone who is successful and humble,' he said once.

Is there any entertainer in the world he admires enough to wish to switch places with at this moment?

'Sure. Prince. But just for one night – he's only five feet three.'

Catch him in a mood to talk and reveal and find out that deep down he does not take acting too seriously, that is, not in that breathless serious way as a calling, a fine, almost-impossible-to-attain art.

'I am an entertainer. I sing and I clown. I'm not an actor. I'm an entertainer and a comedian. I'm not impressed with the whole acting groove. It doesn't blow my mind. What is all this respect for actors? I'm a liar. That's all acting is. I am good at lying . . . Yeah, I tell a good lie . . . '

Said he . . . truthfully.

'One drawback to making it so young is that I have to grow up in the public eye. I say things . . . and two years later I may have grown into another opinion . . . '

He cautions that it is important not to get lost in one's ego, which doesn't mean that one can't enjoy all the things that are happening. He admits freely that he gets 'a big, huge kick' out of seeing himself on a movie screen thirty feet high.

A bit reluctantly, he talks about the art of joke-making.

'To me, that's when all the beauty goes out of comedy, when you analyse it too much . . . '

But he did say in one interview, 'I always like jokes with an edge, a bite to them. Most black comics tend to vent some hostility when they get on stage, anyway, especially in their stand-up. To me, there's a very thin line that a black comic deals with, between becoming the audience's nigger and making the audience hostile. That's the line I like to walk, that's the tension I like to play with. In my stand-up, I love to tease the audience into a trap.'

UNICORNS AND UNDERTAKINGS

What after all is a halo?
It's only one more thing
to keep clean.
—*Christopher Fry*

The whole concept of idolising, of putting halos on some heads, of elevating some to an often unrealistically high level is both an interesting and a double-edged phenomenon.

Movie actors get this kind of adoration more than most others – scientists, writers, painters get less – perhaps because we see them larger than life on that screen. We can actually see them breathe. In some ways, we get closer to them than we do to the real-life people all around us.

We have a need of a little magic in our lives. Perhaps we have a need to believe in unicorns . . . or in the exciting aura around performers.

Often, it is a matter of to what extent we admire and identify and adore.

Eddie Murphy gets lots and lots of adoration.

Many of his colleagues are not surprised. They realise the quality, often called charisma, is real. Some have it, others don't.

Eddie's co-star in *Beverly Hills Cop*, Lisa Eilbacher, is not surprised. She feels that audiences can't help but fall in love with him.

'Because the camera absolutely loves the guy,' she says. 'It's absolutely amazing. He glides where others labour. He takes chances. If it doesn't work, it doesn't. But usually it does. There's something so special about him. Eddie's like a kid that never grew up . . . He has an easiness, an ability to relax with the camera whirring two feet in front of his face.'

Another actor who has worked with him agrees totally and points out that this is the quality the viewers pick up on.

'He totally lacks the perfectly natural fear of the camera, the very thing the rest of us have to work hard to overcome. He's like a small kid learning to ski. He doesn't know that you could break your leg!'

To many, it's almost mystical the way he has succeeded in one of the hardest businesses in the world.

How could a fifteen year old kid tell his parents that he was going to be famous by the time he reached nineteen and a millionaire by the age of twenty-one – and then have exactly that happen to him?!

If one wishes to measure the phenomenal success of Eddie Murphy in money, we may point out that for his first movie (*48 Hrs.*), he was paid 200,000 dollars and it went on to gross around 78 million dollars. His second movie, *Trading Places*, grossed 92.5 million dollars. And *Beverly Hills Cop* is still going strong . . . Magic at work?

Where is he going from here?

The *Cosmopolitan* interviewer asked him where he wanted to be ten years from now.

'By the time I'm thirty, I want to write, produce, direct, star in, and do the score of a movie,' answered Murphy. Then he switched to a joke. 'If I can do that by the time I'm thirty, I'll just become an old Jew and move to Florida (In Yiddish accent) There's notting left for me to do . . . '

There will be movies, probably many, from Eddie Murphy Productions. He may use the company to produce films that he does not star in, too.

He'll go on with and further develop his stand-up routines. This will be enormously interesting as he takes more and more of his material from actual reality as opposed to the earlier television-based stuff.

We have already seen quite a few samples of this. One favourite is his 'Solomon and Pudge' routine about two old bluesmen – the kind of comedy that can bring a tear to your eye – or the skit about Dion, the hairdresser.

He is going to sing, thereby fulfilling his ambition at the age of fifteen when he tried it, then motivated by (he says) the feeling that it would be easier to get girls as a singer than as a joke teller.

Besides, he likes singers, 'Singers are more fun than actors,' he has said, 'because actors take things seriously.'

He is hard at work on his music, often in Stevie Wonder's studio and frequently with the help of Rick James.

He has been writing music for some time now: pop, funk, reggae, various songs . . . (Somebody told about a song with a touch of a hiccuping Elvis Presley.)

He has plans to form a band and take it on the road. He admires David Bowie, whom he calls the 'hippiest' in the business.

'I want to do what he does and tell jokes, too.'

He is definitely going to fulfil the ambition he stated early. 'When I die, I don't want to be stuck back there in a little box among the other obituaries. I want the front page.'

Though we prophesy that he will have many, many headlines before that day comes. What could stop Eddie Murphy now?!

VERY VITAL

Let your life lightly dance
on the edges of time like dew
on the tip of a leaf.
—*Tagore*

Dan Aykroyd admires the way Eddie Murphy takes care of himself.

'His physical vessel is pure. Eddie lives for his work. He's not going to blow his youth and fortune the way so many young performers before him have. Eddie is a virtually untapped reservoir of talent. This guy's going to go on forever.'

He is a high-energy person. He is filled with vitality. He works long hours.

When he hops out of bed, often close to noon since he has a habit of working until the wee hours of the morning, he is not only alive and awake, moving like an athlete, but mentally alert and vital. Interested in everything and anything.

It's as if he habitually skips the dull moments in life.

He seems to be awake and attentive all the time and revitalises as easily as an animal.

He works out regularly in his gym. There is not an ounce of fat on his lean body.

No wonder he seems to like to have his picture taken with his shirt off.

Why shouldn't he show off that body with the slim, strong build?

'And chests sell,' he comments, laughing that crazy laugh again like a lawnmower running over delirious worms and bringing out earth-moving sounds of glee.

Somebody has told us that Eddie Murphy is working on a guide book to the Eddie Murphy life-style – but we don't know if he's kidding.

He is quite aware that a person's health is the key to everything else. What is the use of a fortune if you don't have the health to enjoy it? He learned a lot from his stepfather about the importance of staying in shape and of beginning when you're young because it pays off handsomely in later years.

He has also found that going into the basement and punching the bags relieves pressures and frustrations that otherwise may build up.

No wonder he gets hundreds of letters from women every week, some of them rather explicit about what it is they want from him.

All right, the guy is in great shape and doesn't smoke, drink or do drugs. He goes to nightclubs and when others drink champagne, he asks for a Coke ('no ice, please'). He is a bit fastidious – his friends have said that he doesn't much like to use public rest rooms. But we must also tell his weakness – he does eat junk food sometimes. Pizzas, cinnamon buns, soft drinks such as Coke . . . About the 'finer things' in foods, he has said, 'Anything you have to acquire a taste for was not meant to be eaten.'

WUNDERKIND ... WHITES

Wunderkind ... literally child
of wonder, wonder-child, prodigy ...

Eddie Murphy's movies break box-office records. So
do Richard Pryor's movies.

In other words, two of the absolutely biggest stars of
this decade are black.

That must mean that studios and producers are eager
to discover future black stars and begin to promote them
like crazy. Whenever there is a trend that brings in cash,
it is picked up and followed up on in Hollywood.

They do not.

Is it because Murphy and Pryor are funny?

Is only laughter colour blind?

Here we have a very young black man who already in
1983 was voted the second biggest box-office star of the
year! Number one was Clint Eastwood, a veteran who
has made dozens of movies. Murphy did beat Burt
Reynolds and the rest.

A very young black man who makes fun of anything.
Blacks. Whites. Anyone.

He has a sense of how far he can go (pretty far), at
least most of the time to most of the audiences.

In November of 1982, he performed at the Bayou, a nightclub in Washington, D.C. Outside the streets were still littered with broken glass after violent anti-Ku Klux Klan demonstrations. A mixed audience inside transmitted a certain nervousness.

Eddie sensed everybody's discomfort. So what did he do? He went right into what was on everybody's mind. He started talking about television reports of young blacks looting down-town areas.

'Amazing people, those niggers,' said he. 'They come downtown to protest the Klan and end up stealing bicycles.'

The way he said it, letting the joke hit in all directions at once, the tension in the room melted away.

The poet Ezra Pound has called artists 'the antennae of the race.' Through the media, through what is going on in movies, on television, on the music scene, we can sense which way the wind blows.

'Comedy . . . what makes people laugh and who makes them laugh . . . is significant,' a writer points out. 'When Eddie Murphy gets up there, he gives us what's happening . . . right now . . . not only in his words . . . but in everything he is and represents.'

Who does Eddie Murphy, the man of the hour, attract?

A look at his audience at his stand-up comedy acts reveals that it is mainly a young group, mostly under thirty, and quite evenly balanced between white and black with a healthy sprinkling of 'other.'

Other? Great term that – something Eddie Murphy could have fun with. Like the statistical fact that the population of the United States is 61.2% white, 17% black, and 21.7% other . . .

White? The school system doesn't use that word, of course. They have switched to *Anglo* . . . Oh well, they may have a point – are there any white people outside of powdered clowns and mimes?

What does Eddie Murphy say about his audiences?

He entertains white, black and other with the same gusto.

'My only objective, my only conscious objective, is to make people laugh.'

Yeah, make us laugh, and we'll become more like angels. Laughing from the heart will make us better human beings.

Razor-tongued and quick-witted is he, but it's amazing how he seems to be unaffected by the racism he must have encountered in his own life.

'If somebody called him "nigger" on the street, he just laughed,' says a friend about the high school days.

The place where he lives now is an almost exclusuvely white upper-class town. He says that some neighbours have seemed less than happy but nothing serious. One did complain about the number of cars in the driveway. 'How many people live in this house?'

Eddie thinks that it may be the kind of cars in the driveway that upsets the man rather than anything else.

Another complained about the tennis court lights.

'Again, I think it's the fact that I have a tennis court that's messing with his head.'

He laughs it off.

'It's all such silly stuff.'

With a wisdom far beyond his years, he seems to know that people's power to hurt him is limited by what he allows. Nobody hurts us unless we let ourselves become hurt.

He has said, 'Racism hurts when you don't have, when you're confused and not sure of what you want to do and, on top of that, somebody says you're this and that, which makes you more confused and angry and is an element you don't need in your life. But when you have your feet on the ground, you know what you're doing and what you've got and some truck driver calls you a nigger, you can say, "So what? *You* drive a truck, mutha"!'

He knows he is black, that's part of his persona, part of him as a comic. But he is not an angry young man. He acknowledges his nice suburban middle-class upbringing.

'No poverty, no hunger, no wearing of my big brother's old clothes and shoes,' he told *Players* magazine during an interview.

'I'm not angry,' he told *Newsweek*. 'I didn't learn this stuff hanging out with junkies on 158th Street.'

In the interview in *Players*, he did speculate how it would be to make something like 'Raiders of the Lost Ark' with a black star.

'The media brainwashing is so thorough that we can't imagine black men in these bigger than life roles. I can't imagine a black man running around beating up the bad guys and wearing this giant S on his chest. I would like to write a film like that and see if it could be accepted. I don't think that it's so much overt prejudice as it is a process of conditioning really.

'It would be interesting to see how the public would react to a straight presentation of a black super hero.'

This was said before *Beverly Hills Cop* – in which the lead could have been played by a white or a black man.

He seems to be doing his bit to change the conditioning process.

In many ways, he presents a newer kind of black experience – not coming from ghetto struggle but from everyday middle-class struggle.

He jokes sometimes about differences between black and white ('if God wanted us to be equal, why didn't he give you one of these?!' and he points to a big-size radio). Seriously, he will comment on the differences between black and white audiences. Black audiences are tougher to please, he says.

'Blacks look critically and want to be convinced it is funny; whites tend to come already expecting you to be funny.

'White people don't always know when you're taking

pot shots at them. But it's very hard to make black people laugh. Blacks wouldn't laugh at somebody like Steve Martin wearing a bow and arrow on his head. Blacks just aren't into silly things. You have to do something genuinely funny to make black people laugh.'

X . . . THE UNKNOWN FACTOR

Why, then the world's mine oyster . . .
—*Shakespeare*

What is he like, the hottest funnyman in a long time, the prince of comedy, the irreverent, shocking, brilliant, bawdy, rich, sassy, sexy Eddie Murphy?

What is he really like privately?

He is funny, yes. He keeps doing little impersonations, take-offs . . . he tends to entertain privately just because he so often sees or hears something that triggers his vivid imagination. But he doesn't have a compulsive need to be funny all the time. He can be quiet. He knows how to listen.

He is also a pretty serious fellow, according to all accounts, a guy who likes to ponder things, to understand, to see beneath surfaces.

Is he interested in politics?

He told *Players* in late 1982 that he is not 'a political person, and it doesn't enhance anybody's career to take sides.'

Evidently, there has been some lobbying for his support for candidates and issues.

But is he apolitical?

It does not seem so, and his increasing interest in music is an indication! Yes, he sees music as a good medium im which to express, among other things, political concern.

'See, my comedy is nonpolitical. I want to show that I give a damn, but comedy is the wrong thing to preach with. Eventually, I'll put the music, which is political, into my show,' he stated recently.

Some of the songs he writes are about a world out of control, a world on the brink of the apocalypse . . .

He is the opposite of a superficial person, the person looking for short-cuts in work or in life. He is much aware that it would sometimes be easy to go for the cheap laugh. There is something inside him, weighing and balancing. It is a perilous territory, the land of comedy . . .

He has expressed this himself, showing that he is aware of the dangers of different kinds.

Even if he seems strangely fearless, he is no stranger to fears. He doesn't wear them every day, that's all.

'When I'm in front of the camera, I'm really cocky. I can do anything. But when I'm alone, thinking about things, feeling the business getting the best of me, that's when I get scared. But listen, I figure it's good that I know enough to get away. I won't do no Freddie Prinze deal, pretend the pressures aren't there. I'll never put a bullet in my head.'

He wrote in *Newsweek on Campus:* 'According to tradition, I'm on the road to self-inflicted death . . . I'm supposed to die from drugs, a shot in the head, or a car crash. But I don't do drugs of any kind (never did). I'm afraid of guns (always was). And I'm a damn good driver (always will be). So the only way I'm gonna go is via a plane crash, cancer or a bar room brawl. I don't drink, so why should I be in a bar room? I sincerely hope I don't get cancer. And if I ever go down in a plane, I want to speak into the black box so I can be the only one in history to be taped telling the pilot, "You're an incompetent swine and I hate you." '

He has plenty of confidence, yes. But being the contradiction that is part of the human condition, even Eddie Murphy has his moments of insecurity. Even he asks himself the questions: Am I goodlooking? Am I talented? Can I sing? Am I really funny or is it all a fluke?

Remember, he is a phenomenon and the greatest success of the year, but he is also human. He is, after all, one of us . . . not a creature from another planet . . .

He admits to being a bit manic-depressive . . . either on top of the world or getting into dark moods. Though the latter are infrequent.

He lives with an ambition that is extra large in scope. His mother saw it tearing at him early, at times in an almost painful way.

'I don't ever want to be middle class,' he told her.

Mediocrity scares him.

Does he find solace in religion?

Well, he is a Christian. He prays every night, but he is no fanatic. He has respect for God and church.

In an interview, he said, 'I used to do a lot of God jokes – it's an easy subject for laughs – and my career was going nowhere. I promised God no more God jokes and my career took off.'

He told *Players* magazine: 'I relied on my gift from God to take me where it would.'

He also said, 'I don't follow any particular doctrine; I think religion has been too tampered with, I don't believe that there's any section that's right. I believe in God and I pray to God and I feel that if you know in your heart that you are doing something wrong, then you're centred.'

He is a young man who knows where he is going, but who also knows that he has to keep growing.

Very occasionally, surprisingly seldom, he goes a little crazy at having been thrust into the limelight this early. One time he said, 'If I could change one thing, I'd put off success until thirty years old . . . '

It may feel like that, but there is no way he could have. He is too impatient, too ready to burst into the world.

Anyhow, there's no going back. Only forward . . . and upward . . .

YOUNG IN YEARS BUT . . .

Intellect, talent, and genius,
like murder, 'will out.'
—*C. Simmons*

Are intelligent people funnier????

It takes small effort to observe that Eddie Murphy's intelligence is above average. One definition of intelligence could be the ability to perceive things, often unsaid and unexplained things, and draw conclusions from them.

That is his speciality!

Born in 1961, he is a definite product of the television age. If it hasn't been on TV, chances are he won't know about it. He is hazy on subjects such as geography, history, biology . . . but what he knows, he knows definitely and with clarity.

'Eddie's like a sponge,' his manager says. 'He picks up anything.'

'If I like a movie, I can give it back to you scene by scene, with all the dialogue and shots,' Eddie admits.

We are aware that he was less than brilliant in grammar and high school. Not interested, is probably a better definition.

He claims that he has read only one book straight through (Salinger's *Catcher in the Rye*) and only one school subject really fascinated him (astronomy).

Other than that . . . well . . . he wrote in *Newsweek on Campus*, 'I hated school. I was terrible in school. I learned the basics: how to read, write and add. I cut class. I was a prankster.'

Now, only a few years later, he has three hit movies and two gold comedy albums (one won a Grammy) behind him.

Does that mean that being a poor student promises success in life?

Only if you have a gift that is so shining and unique that all else doesn't matter . . . and if you have the willingness to keep learning much harder than in school every day the rest of your life . . .

Walter Hill (the director of *48 Hrs.*) says about Eddie, 'He has a remarkably strong centre, a strong feeling for who he is . . . Remarkable indeed . . . and he's so young . . . '

Martin Brest (director of *Beverly Hills Cop*) says, 'He's simply a movie star. He has a sexiness, a brilliant sense of humour allied with intelligence. He doesn't have to ham it up, because he's so intelligent. You read that in his eyes, and he becomes riveting.'

Newsweek claimed already a couple of years ago that the only reason anybody with a mental age above twelve could bear to watch *Saturday Night Live* was – Eddie Murphy.

Young but with a centre.

'Show business is my dream come true and I don't want to do anything else in life in terms of a profession. The only other thing I want out of life is a family and that'll happen in its own time,' he told *Players* magazine.

ZEST AND ZEAL

Zeal is the fire of love . . .

In person, Eddie Murphy projects an unmistakable star aura.

People recognise him on streets, in stores, in elevators . . . and they blink and quiver a little as if they had just received a series of electric shocks.

He walks into a restaurant and heads swivel.

He walks onto a stage, and there's a buzz increasing to a near delirium.

We all know that success and fame destroy, right?

There are horror stories galore on the subject.

Picasso once said that he wouldn't wish fame on his worst enemy.

Fame may create expectations that can far exceed the capacity of an artist in his struggle to deliver.

But in the case of Eddie Murphy . . . he just seems to enjoy it to the hilt!

'It's fun being rich, famous and getting love from millions of people!'

Celebrities are known to have fragile egos and live with

114

constant insecurity. But not Murphy. He moves happily along.

And he's confident that his best work is yet to come!

When he talks about himself and his career, he compares himself strangely enough not to his contemporaries, the meteors that flashed across and burned themselves out, often shockingly, tragically. No, he compares himself to oldtime veterans such as Charlie Chaplin and Bob Hope . . .

Charlie Chaplin . . . the man who made the world laugh during hard times. Things are hard again . . . what happens when life gets difficult? People want to laugh!

Eddie Murphy is aware of this. 'The country is not in a wild and crazy mood . . . People seem frustrated . . . uncomfortable . . . A lot of their laughter is nervous laughter. Some comedy is quite disgusting . . . the movies are filled with violence . . . I want to hear people really, really laugh!'

And he is going to keep on doing his utmost to make that happen.

He is well aware of the drawbacks to fame. 'Maybe I miss going to the mall, hanging out, stuff like that. But when you weigh the two, I'd rather be an entertainer.'

But as his face is more and more known, it gets worse.

After his films, his concerts, being on at least three editions of Johnny Carson's *Tonight* show, having co-hosted the 35th Annual Emmy Awards telecast with Joan Rivers, having been a presenter at the Oscars, the Emmys, the Grammys, having appeared on other talk-shows, having been forced to cancel record-signing parties because of the crush of fans, having received the NAACP Image Award as Best Actor in a Motion Picture, and Emmy nominations, he is not exactly Mr. Anonymous.

He has complained. 'I have no privacy at all. It used to be that I couldn't walk down the street in peace. Now

I'm followed by people even when I go for a drive. They want to pull over and talk.'

But his complaints are overshadowed by his willingness to do what he does, to work as hard as it takes and then some.

It also helps that he genuinely likes people. Even cynical reporters come from meetings with Eddie Murphy with awe-struck faces and big grins.

'That charisma and the warmth he exudes on stage and screen is *real*,' is a commonly heard comment.

Dan Aykroyd stated it simply in *Rolling Stone* magazine in the beginning of 1983:

'1983 is the year of Eddie Murphy.'

So was 1984, so is 1985 . . . and on it goes.

Eddie Murphy, a man of zest and zeal who loves what he is doing, is on his way to become the youngest legend ever. He has revealed that his ambition is to be identified with the 80's as Elvis Presley is identified with the 50's, and the Beatles with the 60's. We know from his past history what happens when Eddie Murphy states an ambition: *Boom! Zap!* The ambition becomes a fact!

He laughs, and we hear a heartbeat in his laughter as his big eyes reflect the glorious future spreading out, unfolding like a peacock's studded tail.

EDDIE MURPHY
AND NUMEROLOGY:
ACCORDING TO
PYTHAGORAS . . .

The Greek scientist Pythagoras (c.582-c.507 B.C.) advanced the theory that numbers constitute the true nature of things.

He held that all relationships – even abstract ethical concepts – could be expressed numerically.

According to his mathematics as philosophy, a science, today popularly known as numerology, developed.

Following Pythagorean principles as strictly as possible, using Eddie Murphy's complete given name (Edward Regan Murphy) and his birthdate (April 3, 1961), some astonishing revelations are made.

The name given at birth plays a big part. Each vowel and each consonant has a vibration, corresponding to a mathematical symbol. The letters will indicate talents and qualities that the person came to the world with. The numbers constituting the date of birth represent what the person has to do in the world as well as challenges to be met.

117

Free will exists. Any quality emphasised by the numbers can be used one of three ways: positively, negatively, or destructively.

From the 'number values,' it is clear that we are here dealing with a person with a *special destiny*.

A fine, important period is coming up in his life, but it is also a time when various forces, within and without, may try to pull him in different directions.

He must not listen to anyone on the outside at this time. It is of extreme importance that he only listens to and trusts totally his own intuition. This was emphasised in several ways. He must follow his instincts, trust his intuition – somehow, he knows better than anyone else what is best for him.

If he follows what he intuitively picks up, if he is sensitive to the existing 'vibes,' he will choose the right projects and activities.

A strong presence of number 7 (the holy number in the cabala, the number of silence) as well as the number 22 (one of the master numbers) is noted.

He is both the architect and the builder of his life and career.

He can have a tremendous influence on his surroundings, even on the world. He should develop plans on a grand scale, mentally speaking, to use this influence – his main duty is to influence others. He could even become a kind of world ambassador.

If anything *feels* wrong to him, he should not do it.

It is advised that he learn to develop a quiet patience with himself. He is so filled – to the point of overflowing – with talents of many kinds that he needs to seek a quiet place and 'sort himself out' from time to time.

Nobody should influence him, not in important matters. He has great powers, and he must be careful how he uses them. Nobody should try to use his power, to exploit him – nobody should try to take anything but inspiration from him.

Words play a major part in his life. He will always be able to express himself in words, written, spoken or sung. (Music is of deep significance in the Pythagorean system of thought.)

He has a magnetic personality and will automatically be in the centre of things.

He must focus his energies in order not to dissipate them.

He has a strong interest in metaphysical and philosophical matters.

Whatever he does, it must never be only for himself. He has a duty, a responsibility to society.

He should watch a tendency toward stubbornness in the extreme.

Another thing for him to watch is a tendency to becoming overpowering, which would affect partnerships (this would include emotional relationships and marriage). He should learn a softer approach at times.

Part of his learning task is to learn about his own emotions.

His creativity is nearly boundless. He could write tremendous and important things. (Had he chosen another path and worked as hard in that direction, he could have become a physician, specifically a surgeon.)

He could be instrumental in really changing attitudes in society.

He ought to, as time goes on, take a more active part in education and in direct contact with young people. He is needed by young and old in a culture that has gone astray.

He is an educator without knowing it, what mystics tend to call 'an old soul' (which is why school held little interest to him – he already knew so many things), a person with a rich inner world.

He has all the capacities and qualities of the leader, but he must learn to rule wisely.

He has been given talents in just about every area in

tremendous measure. He should remain true to his ideals.

He has tremendous drive, but he need not strive to get power: It has been given to him. He could surpass just about anyone in his field.

He will never have to worry about financial security as long as he lives.

There are no negative qualities in him, nothing bad – unless he would choose to use his powers destructively.

To use his energy most effectively, it would be well if he did not reveal plans before they are definite. It would be to his advantage not to talk too much about things before they materialise. Chances are that he has a natural tendency to keep quiet about the specifics of planned ventures, and this is good.

He has been born to do good, and he will, as he trusts his tremendous, almost uncanny intuition and sees his special responsibilities clearly.

EDDIE MURPHY'S PERSONAL HOROSCOPE BORN APRIL 3, 1961

Sun in Aries (13 degrees)
Ruled by Mars, the sun gives much mental energy and a quick wit. A natural leader, headstrong & impulsive. Ambitious, full of enterprise and new and original ideas. It is not likely that this person can be controlled by others. He is fiery and quick-tempered, likely to be rash and hasty in speech. However, he resents abuse, both of himself and others. But he is also forgiving and will not hold a grudge for long. He possesses a great love of freedom and justice. Combined with his strong self-will, this makes him likely to go to extremes. Lacks discretion because of his hasty speech. He is persistent and not easily discouraged. At his best when he is in control of things.

Moon in Scorpio (10 degrees, approximate)
The person is strong-willed, determined, and practical. Possesses the self-confidence to succeed in whatever he undertakes. He may be abrupt and impulsive, will not

tolerate imposition from others. He is energetic, forceful, independent, aggressive, courageous and positive in his approach to things. Ruled by Pluto, his moon makes him fond of pleasure and comfort, giving him the need to satisfy all sensual appetites. He is also generous and will sacrifice to return a kindness. He is quick-tempered, and uses sarcasm and satire with the objective of accomplishing revolutionary changes. He is strongly attracted to the opposite sex, and attractive to the opposite sex, but he suffers many difficulties with women.

Mercury in Pisces (19 degrees)

Knowledge is gained not by deep study but by intuition. His understanding may be deep, but it is not gained through books. He has a peculiar or original view of things as a result. His mind is imaginative, impressional, and quickly adapts to the needs of the moment. Has a capacity to absorb knowledge and a good ability to memorise. He is fond of pleasure, recreation, and travelling, especially on water. (This tends to place him in danger at times). He is multi-talented, and may change employment frequently or engage in several businesses simultaneously. He is a good judge of human nature, is analytical, cautious, fair, good-humoured and versatile.

Venus in Aries (25 degrees)

This person has a fondness for travel and for the arts, as well as for romance, adventure, and entertainment. He is affectionate and demonstrative with his affection. He is fond of being loved and admired, is warm-hearted, passionate, and attracts friends of the opposite sex. Likely to be extremely popular, attracting many friends. He is free and generous with money and gifts, and will respond to appeals for assistance from friends.

Mars in Cancer (14 degrees)

This person is ambitious and hard-working, fearless and

bold. However, he may have sudden outbursts of temper
and tendencies to irritability. He is fond of luxury and
sensual pleasures. Original and independent, he rebels
against authority. Gains through business travel and
through concerns of a public nature. Success may require
physical effort. He is also changeable. There is a
possibility that he suffered a separation from a parent.
He may change residence with some frequency, and will
suffer trouble in home life, possibly a discontented
marriage partner. Tendency to accidents in his home, and
may suffer danger from water, earthquakes, and theft.

Jupiter in Aquarius (3 degrees)
This person is cheerful, good-humoured, obliging, just,
compassionate, sympathetic, and philanthropic. He
dislikes discord and disharmony. He is intuitive, refined,
liberal, and philosophical by nature. Interested in new
ideas, social concerns, and reform of institutions.
Engages in pursuits that are out of the ordinary. In his
own views, he is original, independent, and progressive.
He may be indifferent to the ordinary affairs of life,
seeking to develop his higher mind. He benefits through
good and sincere friends, who are gained by his personal
magnetism.

Saturn in Capricorn (28 degrees)
Saturn in its own sign gives the person a tendency
towards seriousness, caution, suspicion, and discontent.
(However, note that it is conjunct Jupiter). He is
acquisitive by nature, both with money and possessions.
He is a deep thinker and a good reasoner. He is
ambitious and is anxious – even impatient – to rise in
life. He succeeds through tact, diplomacy, and persistence.
He may be attracted to those of lesser station in life and
may at times attract unreliable friends. May experience
ups and downs in career – failure following success, but
succeeding again through persistence and effort.

Uranus in Leo (21 degrees)
The person is of an industrious mentality. Although he is at times headstrong, fiery, and eccentric, he is generally disposed to physical moderation. He disregards conventionality, and is of a rebellious disposition, which often results in suffering disfavour from others. He cannot tolerate being given orders or being contradicted. Has a great love for freedom and independence. Likes adventure, and possesses some strange or peculiar attractions and tendencies. There may be some odd or unusual experiences with affections and love affairs, with some sorrow or estrangement as a result. May experience obstacles in home life in his youth, and some difficulty or loss connected with his father.

Neptune in Scorpio (10 degrees)
The person has intense feelings and emotions, and a great ability for inventiveness and originality. He is persistent and quick-tempered, but has some tendencies toward secrecy and reserve. Extreme love of luxury, and sensual things, and may suffer as a result. He may suffer slander, rebuke, and losses through the treachery of friends and associates.

Pluto in Virgo (6 degrees)
He pays much attention to detail and is concerned about health and service to society. Tendency to experiment with diet. Dislikes food additives, prefers natural or pure foods; may turn to vegetarianism at some point. Concern for exercise and weight-maintenance, and may be attracted to Yoga, or meditation. Has an inventive and original mind; seeks new forms of communication to the masses.

PLANETARY ASPECTS

Moon Trine Mars
The person is ambitious, energetic, firm, brave, and

resolute. Has a strong and healthy body, inclined to much activity and vitality. He finds success through his own resourcefulness and enterprise, and likely to be in a position of high responsibility or public honour. He gets results through quick action, common sense, and hard work. May gain through the mother, if not financially then through inherited traits. This is a good aspect for friendship, group associates, property, and gaining of hopes and wishes.

Moon Conjunct Neptune

Possesses a strong imagination, highly artistic. May succeed in fields of art, writing, speaking, or acting. Likes watery activities – boating, swimming, etc. Likes pleasing the public, may be involved in film and mass entertainment, and can succeed in these ambitions. There may be a danger from alcohol, drugs, or water – or friends and associates involved with them. This can work one of two ways – may succumb to the dangers or may develop a strong aversion because he is aware of the dangers.

Mercury trine Mars

The person is quick, lively, bright, alert, witty, humorous, satirical, and ingenious. A very good aspect for an entertainer, but also for a businessman. He is constructive, practical, skilful, and businesslike. He is generally enthusiastic, animated, with a magnetic personality. Forceful and enterprising. Highly developed mind. Has artistic abilities – drawing, music, carving, designing, acting, etc. Is associated with literary and professional people.

Venus trine Uranus

Possesses a fondness and an ability for the fine arts, but tends toward new or radical departures from the traditional. He possesses an attractive, magnetic personality that gains many friends and acquaintances. He will find success through these associates. This is a fortunate aspect for business success as well as artistic success. His mind is bright, quick, intuitive, and inspirational. He benefits through fraternal, social or progressive groups, but also through strangers or peculiar or unexpected circumstances. The opposite sex is greatly attracted to him, and he has friends among artists, inventors, politicians, and unusual or extraordinary persons.

Venus Square Saturn
He may suffer disappointment and trouble in courtship and marriage, and in partnership. At times, he may also suffer public censure, unpopularity, or disapproval. Interference, or misfortune may occur through elders, parents, or relatives. There is a tendency also to suffer dangers through deception, jealousy of others, or from theft. Excessive sensuality may also pose problems. Marriage will probably be delayed until after age 28, and it may prove a difficult one, possibly because of differences in age, social position or financial matters. However, he is of a diplomatic nature and will make every effort to overcome problems. He may suffer some business losses as a result of speculation, bad investments in lands, mines, companies, and banks.

Sun Square Mars
The person has many ups and down in his career. He faces continual obstacles in the path of his desires. His impulsiveness, pride, and anger may cause difficulties, resulting in separations, enmities, and litigations. Possibility of an early death of the father, or at least a separation from him. He has a hasty, fiery temper, though it is not lasting. Extremely ambitious, but does not always have the self-confidence and patience to see a project through to success. He is outspoken, assertive, aggressive, combative, impulsive, forceful, sometimes

126

overbearing and destructive. As a result, he can tend to lose the esteem of superiors and those in high position, and so must guard against his impulsiveness. May suffer sudden sharp attacks of sickness, cuts, burns and scalds.

Jupiter Conjunct Saturn
This is a good aspect for financial affairs and for possessions. It also aids inventiveness and ingenuity and gives a strongly practical nature, in relation to career, occupation, and the public. He possesses good mental ability, with a capacity for learning. He also has the strength of character and the personal power to overcome obstacles. He is serious, profound, and philosophical, and succeeds with elders and those in high positions. He has sound judgment because of an ability to appraise, compare, concentrate, and arbitrate. He has a strong sense of justice; he also possesses sincerity, honesty, and thrift, and will attract esteem and general prosperity. A favourable aspect for money and possessions.

GENERAL COMMENTS

Retrogrades
There are four retrograde planets in this chart (Venus, Uranus, Neptune, and Pluto). As a general rule, the fewer retrograde planets, the more one is inclined to accept circumstances and not fight to overcome them. The more retrogrades, the more obstacles, but also the more likelihood of overcoming them and achieving 'earned' success. Statistically, four retrogrades generally signifies success in writing or in the mass media – that which is related to communcation. The person will be good with words, rational thought, and communication with the public.

Venus Retrograde – generally makes social activities difficult for the person, inclining him toward solitude or living alone. He has to work at overcoming this tendency to acquire a social life.

Uranus Retrograde – gives a respect for traditional methods and values, but an ingenuity required to alter them subtly. Necessary to overcome a basic insecurity and lack of self-confidence with his own new ideas. A desire for public acceptance.

Neptune Retrograde – makes pretence or lying difficult, an aversion to drugs and alcohol, and an impatience with those dependent upon them. Must work at overcoming excessive honesty to accept imagination and dissimulation.

Pluto Retrograde – gives a raw power and a willingness to employ it to have a widespread effect upon the masses. Obstacles to overcome in sexuality and revolutionary or rebellious ideas.

ELEMENTS

Planetary placements are heavily in Water signs, which tends to cool down some of this otherwise fiery chart. This cooling often results in steam, however. While he is able to 'go with the flow' of his water planets, he is not always happy about it – stewing and steaming with impatience. However, he should realise that the delays help prevent him from burning himself out. He has some planets in earth signs, which give him some 'grounding.' He has little in air signs, though, and this keeps him from 'intellectual' or 'dreamlike' pursuits. He is essentially 'action' oriented.

NATURE & CHARACTER

The planets of this chart are heavily in Cardinal signs, which reemphasises the action nature of the person, though Mutable signs run a close second. This person sets out to achieve goals, and is rarely satisfied until those goals are achieved. He has few planets in the stubborn Fixed signs, and so achieves a balance between 'rushing in where angels fear to tread' and adapting himself to the needs of the moment, or to circumstances he can't control.

RULERSHIP

Only one planet in this chart is in the sign it rules, and that is Saturn, which is in Capricorn. This emphasises the practical, businesslike nature of the person. It makes him acquisitive, both in money and possessions, and gives him a serious attitude, with an emphasis on matters of occupation, the public, and career. The Ruler of the Chart is Pluto (which itself is ruled by Mercury). Pluto emphasises the intuitive nature of this individual. He operates largely on the basis of instinct – subconsciously. He wants to affect the masses in some revolutionary way, and he does it by his 'words,' by communication through writing, acting, mass media. To some extent, there is a sexuality inherent in whatever he does. He is attractive, and he uses his attraction to accomplish his ends, as well as generally to his own benefit.

His sun is ruled by Mars (which is in turn ruled by the Moon), and this gives his nature an active, energetic, always moving appearance. Very masculine, he would do well in a career involving the military or the police, or any requiring athletics or action.

His Moon is ruled by Pluto, which indicates that he prefers to keep his true emotions unseen, below the surface. These emotions are strongly linked to women and to sex; his mother was probably a strong influence in his life. Women generally are important to him, but he prefers to keep them out of his public life, to keep his affairs and friendships secret.

Neptune is also ruled by Pluto, and this tends to reinforce the above. It also adds creativity and a strong subconscious intuition to film work, acting, music, and any 'imaginative' effort he undertakes.

Mercury is ruled by Neptune, and for this reason his communication is best achieved through film. (He might even have a talent for film writing.) He probably enjoys travelling on water. And he is excellent at conveying emotions.

Venus is ruled by Mars, which makes romance and marriage difficult. The lover or marriage partner attempts to control this individual, which can't be done. He cannot permit anyone to 'hold him down.' This factor also emphasises the 'masculine' roles he will portray in his art. It also gives him the appearance of being a 'male chauvinist,' though the truth is that he always has to lead the way and let others follow, whatever their sex.

SIGNIFICANT PERIODS, BY PROGRESSION

Progressed New Moon occurred at age 12 in 1973. This would have been a significant year for him. (Could have occurred six months before his birthday.) In some way, this would have signified a beginning for his ambitions, setting himself on the course he would be following for the next fourteen to fifteen years. Generally this is a 'career' decision, but dependent on the house placement of his sun and moon, it can also relate to other phases of the individual's life. In this case I believe it to be directed toward Career and toward family or home situation. At age 12, the native would have set himself on a course in these two spheres, which will culminate with the *Progressed Full Moon* at age 27, in 1988. The native will have achieved all he set out to accomplish by this time. He will have reached all his ambitions for his career at this time, and very likely will marry around this time. (Or

130

at least achieve the home situation he desires.)

For a person with as much drive as this individual, the years that follow may seem to some extent a 'let-down.' He will feel he is coasting on his past accomplishments. While he may continue to experience as much success, he will not feel himself 'progressing.' (This dissatisfaction could have a negative effect on his home life or marriage.)

This will be compounded by the fact that his *Progressed Uranus* will turn direct the preceding year (1987). His mind will become more erratic and more volatile. He will actually become much more creative than before, but it will take some time to adjust to his less 'conservative' approach to his art. While he is adjusting, those around him will be highly critical, and there will be much negative publicity. It is possible that both sexual partners and business partners will come and go for a time. At a pinnacle of success, he will be frustrated that (it seems) there is no higher he can go, and he will take out his frustrations on others – on those closest to him.

Some changes in personality and mental attitude take place by progression. This person's *Progressed Sun Changed Signs* at age 17, in 1978. While his Aries nature did not leave him at this time, he did begin to acquire some of the attributes of Taurus. He became somewhat more stubborn, affectionate, down-to-earth. More practical and 'home-loving,' as well as more acquisitive – both in money and in possessions. He also acquired a greater sense of art and/or aesthetic appreciation, perhaps more appreciative of nature itself.

His *Progressed Mercury has Changed Signs* twice. The first change occured at age 7, approximately in 1968. (This is always give-or-take six months). This first Mercury change was from the sign Pisces to the sign Aries. At this time he became less placid and accepting mentally of the things occurring in his home environment. While he may have been rather dreamy or introverted as a small child, he suddenly became almost angry. There would have been fights with parents and siblings; he would have become much more outspoken and sure of himself, standing up for himself at least verbally if not physically.

The second Mercury change took place in 1985 (perhaps six months before his birthday, which would be 1984). This change was from Aries to Taurus, and the overall effect would be to 'calm' his vigorous, combative, agile mind. The verbal and mental 'fighting' approach he has been taking since age 7 is over, and he now adjusts to a more loving approach to communication. The desire for marriage and a home-life will be in his mind more often in the coming years. His mind will be more fertile, and he will have a greater sense of the aesthetic. He may turn to writing, discovering that he has this ability, not just for scenes of action and excitement, but for gentle and quiet beauty as well. In his personal life, he finds he is better able to understand the true meaning of love, and he becomes more appreciative of women. He will, as a result, become less 'chauvinistic.'

EDDIE SHARES BIRTHDAY
WITH MARLON AND DORIS

That's right. Marlon Brando (born 1924) and Doris Day (born as Doris von Kappelhoff, also 1924) share Eddie's birthday, April 3.

Quite a number of other celebrities have the fortune to be born on that day.

From the field of baseball, there are Art Ditmas (born 1929), Alex Grammas (born 1927), and Wally Moon (born 1930). Earl Lloyd from basketball, and football players Lyle Martin Alzado (1949), Jim Parker (1934), and Russ Francis (1953), hockey players Bernie Parent (1945) and William Fraser Dea (1933), golfers Phil

Rodgers (1938), Sandra Ann Spuzick (1937) and Rod Funseth (1933).

The auto racer Speedy Thompson (1926) and the astronaut Virgil Ivan Grisson (1926) share the day.

So do author Washington Irving (*Rip Van Winkle, Legend of Sleepy Hollow* – he was born 1783!), famed publisher Henry Luce (1898), and the comedian George Jessel (1898).

From the acting profession, there are Marsha Mason (1942), singer/actor Wayne Newton (1942), singer Tony Orlando (1944), actress Jan Sterling (1923), actress Miyoshi Umeki (1929), and singer/musician Don Gibson (1928)

MOVE OVER, BURT . . .
EDDIE MURPHY IS
CLEARLY TOPS AMONG
MALE STARS

For almost fifty years, there has been a conclusive indicator of who is on top among performers: Boxoffice Magazine's Star Poll. This poll is the result of ballots mailed in by about 400 of the magazine's 15,000 subscribers (primarily film exhibitors).

Burt Reynolds has been in the elite group of stars for five consecutive years, sharing the No. 1 spot with Clint Eastwood in 1980 and winning outright in 1981 and 1982.

In the latest poll (for 1984), Eddie Murphy is clearly tops among male stars, followed by Bill Murray, Clint Eastwood, and Harrison Ford. (On the female side, Sally Field is the Top Female Attraction, with Goldie Hawn, Kathleen Turner, and Meryl Streep right behind.)

Clint Eastwood reigned in 1983, followed by Murphy, Reynolds and Jack Nicholson (queens that year were Streep, Shirley MacLaine, Barbra Streisand, and Debra Winger).

THE FILMS OF EDDIE MURPHY

Following a brief apprenticeship as a stand up comedian in clubs in and around New York, Eddie Murphy became an overnight sensation on *Saturday Night Live*. From television, the natural progression was to films. In his short and meteoric career, Murphy has made only four films. A brief synopsis of each follows:

TRADING PLACES

The film begins with a bet between two elderly, eccentric brothers, the Duke brothers (Ralph Bellamy and Don Ameche.) They have been discussing which is most important: heredity or environment.

They decide to make an experiment.

They pick up Billy Ray Valentine (Eddie Murphy), a black con man who is presently begging on the street pretending to be a blind and legless Vietnam veteran. They install him in an elegant town house with a servant (Denholm Elliott), give him a position in their commodities brokerage firm and a salary of $80,000 a year.

They also fire Valentine's predecessor, Louis Winthrope III (Dan Aykroyd), manipulate things so that his engagement is broken, humiliate him in front of his peers, destroy his credit rating and see to it that his bank accounts are frozen.

They have made the two trade places. Now, they sit back to see how each of them will cope with his totally new position in life.

The result: Well, the brother who believes that environment is more important than genetic factors clearly wins!

Billy Ray Valentine is stunned at first but quickly recovers and fits into his new life as a rich, influential man. He makes money for the firm (in pork bellies) and learns how one behaves and talks in high society.

Louis Winthrope III, for his part, goes downhill fast and ends up making an appearance at the firm's Christmas party, dressed as Santa Claus, while trying to steal a whole smoked salmon.

Billy Ray, however, overhears a remark and discovers the plot of the Duke Brothers. He and Winthrope get together and decide to get even with the brothers for playing God.

They enlist the help of the servant who works for Billy Ray as well as that of a whore with a heart of gold (Jamie Lee Curtis), who has taken pity on Winthrope. Together these four engineer a trading coup on the floor of the New York Commodities Exchange that earns them millions and leaves the Duke brothers totally ruined.

48 HRS.

Jack Cates (Nick Nolte) has been on the San Francisco police force for fifteen years but never made it past detective.

He answers a call that seems to be routine concerning stolen credit cards. Suddenly the shooting begins, and two policemen are dead. Cates identifies the killer as an escaped convict. He and his partner have already killed a prison guard.

In order to find these two, he turns to Reggie Hammond (Eddie Murphy) for help. Reggie used to be a member of the same gang as the killers but is presently in prison, serving time for robbery.

Reggie agrees to help, but we find out he will do so only because he knows about the half a million dollars that is hidden in the trunk of a car. Reggie is released from jail for forty-eight hours to help Cates.

Jack and Reggie make an 'odd couple': Reggie is black, hip, smooth-talking . . . Jack is white, gruff and ready to fight at any time.

During the movie, respect and trust grows between the two as they set out to search for the killers, picking up various clues and finally reaching a showdown.

BEST DEFENCE

Dudley Moore plays Wylie Cooper, an engineer, habitually plagued by bad luck, who accidentally gets hold of a crucial part of the Army's new supertank.

He becomes the resident genius and saviour of the failing defence plant where he works. His bosses hope to get a government contract out of all this. An international industrial spy is after the secret and the FBI is after the spy.

The story of engineer Cooper is intercut with sequences set two years later in the deserts of Kuwait, where Eddie Murphy as Lieutenant Landry is in charge of testing the Annihilator Tank.

We are supposed to be on the edge of our seats, wondering whether Murphy's tank, equipped with the possibly defective crucial part, will self-destruct.

The two characters, played by Moore and Murphy in this political satire or attempted such, do not ever meet.

In the end, both of them, each in their place, choose to act heroically, rather than take the easy way out and look the other way.

BEVERLY HILLS COP

Detroit Police Officer Axel Foley (Eddie Murphy) is in steamingly hot water when a self-assigned undercover scheme to catch a cigarette smuggling ring backfires, wreaking havoc all around.

His colleagues kid him, and his boss, Inspector Todd (Gilbert Hall) is furious, because this is one more in a series of incidents where young Axel Foley's enthusiasm for law enforcement has outweighed his judgment.

At the end of the unusually rough day, Foley is happy to find his old friend Mikey (James Russo) waiting for him.

Mikey, who has been working in Beverly Hills, California, shows Axel a wad of valuable (and untraceable) bearer bonds, but Axel, the policeman, does not want to know anything about his childhood pal's illegal activities. They spend an evening together remembering the old days, having fun, reaffirming a close and good friendship. Then they come back to Axel's place. Hiding in the hallways are Zack Danton (Jonathan Banks) and Casey (Michael Champion). They take Axel and Mikey by surprise, knock Axel unconscious and murder Mikey. We realise that the killing has something to do with the bearer bonds in Mikey's possession.

Axel is filled with sorrow. He is also confused . . . and angry . . . and he does not take it well when he is told that he is not allowed to participate in the investigation.

He asks for vacation time instead. His boss forces a promise from him not to interfere with the investigation. He is too personally involved, his boss feels.

Axel sets out for Beverly Hills in his old car.

It's his first trip to California. He laughs out loud at some things, looks with amazement at the 'Beverly Hills chic' all around him.

He checks into an elegant and expensive hotel, not raising an eyebrow when he discovers the daily rate.

He goes to a fancy art gallery run by Jeannette Summers (Lisa Eilbacher), a childhood friend from Detroit of both Axel and Mikey. She is thrilled to see Axel and terribly upset to hear the news of their friend's murder. She is the one who was instrumental in convincing her boss, Victor Maitland (Steven Berkoff) to hire Mikey as a guard in the gallery's warehouse.

When Axel hears this, he sets out for the offices of wealthy Victor Maitland. Zack, one of the murderers, is with Maitland, but Axel didn't have a chance to see Zack the night of the killing. A band of security men expel the T-shirted Detroit policeman (he never reveals this fact), right through a huge glass window. The Beverly Hills cops arrive and arrest Axel. They bring him to the Beverly Hills Police Department – quite different from the Detroit ditto.

Officers Taggard (John Ashton) and Rosewood (Judge Reinhold) ask why Axel didn't identify himself as a police officer. They state that six witnesses testified he broke into a private office, tore the place up and jumped through a window. The interrogation goes downhill until Taggart in a moment of fury strikes Axel. Chief of Detectives Lt. Bogomil (Ronny Cox) becomes furious.

Then he relays a message from Axel's superior in Detroit to absolutely stay out of the murder investigation.

Axel is let go against bail (Jeannette bails him out).

Bogomil orders Taggart and Rosewood to tail this obviously troublesome and certainly unorthodox Detroit cop.

Jeannette is upset that Axel has bothered her boss Maitland; however, Axel is an old friend.

As she drives him back to the hotel, Axel discovers that there is a tail on him. He orders two fancy meals and sends those out to Taggart and Rosewood in the police car outside the hotel. He sneaks out and deposits a banana in the tailpipe, as well.

This way he can get away before they discover what is wrong and can follow. He tells Jeannette that he is determined to solve Mikey's murder, and he convinces her to allow him inside Maitland's warehouse.

Hidden, the two of them observe two guards unload a truck that holds hidden bonds of the same kind Mikey had. They follow the guards to another building near the airport. Axel comments that it appears that Jeannette's employer is involved in some interesting business ventures.

He sends Jeannette home and poses as a customs official in order to follow the box the Maitland men have dropped off and to learn the inner workings of the U.S. Customs operation. Meanwhile, Taggart and Rosewood wait at Axel's hotel.

Upon returning to the hotel, Axel convinces them to join him at a strip joint. This is against their orders, but they are supposed to tail him, and he is very convincing. In the club, they – mainly Axel – foil a holdup. The club is outside the Beverly Hills jurisdiction, so Bogomil is upset.

He assigns another pair of policemen to follow the difficult Axel, who has a room service breakfast sent to their unmarked car.

Then Axel manages to lose the tailing policemen as he follows Maitland's automobile to a private club. Outrageously, he talks his way into the exclusive place and confronts Maitland and Zack. He disposes of Zack and exchanges threats with Maitland. The Beverly Hills Police are again called to arrest Axel, while Maitland orders Zack to 'take care' of the Detroit pest without delay.

At police headquarters, Axel informs Lt. Bogomil that Maitland is into smuggling and that he knows how the operation works. He has no definite proof, but he is convinced that Maitland, the prominent Beverly Hills citizen, had Mikey murdered. The police order Axel to leave town.

Maitland and Zack interrogate Jeannette about her Detroit friend, but she reveals next to nothing.

Rosewood has been instructed to escort Axel out of town. But Rosewood, a naive, likeable, honest man, has grown to like Axel and allows him to stop at the art gallery to see Jeannette.

Axel, Rosewood, and Jeannette go on to the warehouse, where another shipment is due. Rosewood waits outside while Axel and Jeannette find a crate with hidden drugs just before they are apprehended by Casey (the other murderer) and another Maitland thug.

Rosewood is confused when he sees Jeannette escorted out of the building into a car. Against all rules, he enters and ultimately saves Axel.

Rosewood and Axel then rush to Maitland's estate (Rosewood has radioed Taggart on the way – Taggart is sure he's up to something stupid). Taggart arrives and attempts to arrest Axel, but Axel uses his powers of persuasion again and finally, Axel and the two policemen enter the grounds.

Back at the Beverly Hills Police Department, Bogomil discovers (through the wonders of electronics) that one of his cars is at the Maitland estate.

As the millionaire's tough security force violently battles the three cops, the Beverly Hills Police are on their way. During the shoot-out, Maitland shoots Axel in the shoulder and uses Jeannette as a shield in an escape attempt.

It is utter bloody chaos in the posh neighbourhood.

In the end, the good guys win. Mikey's murder is solved. A major crime syndicate headed by Maitland is wiped out (all of this in a couple of days).

Axel checks out of his hotel. Just then Taggart and Rosewood arrive to pay his bill on behalf of a grateful Beverly Hills Police Department.

But they have also been ordered to escort him all the way to the city limits . . .